Accelerated Learning

*How To Effortlessly Learn Any Skill
Or Subject, Double Your Reading Speed And
Develop Laser Sharpe Focus And Memory –
Instantly – OUT-THINK ANYONE*

Table Of Contents

Introduction

I want to thank you and congratulate you for downloading the book, "*Accelerated Learning: How To Effortlessly Learn Any Skill Or Subject, Double Your Reading Speed And Develop Laser Sharpe Focus And Memory – Instantly – OUT-THINK ANYONE*

You may not believe this but you are twice as smart as you think! The five simple actions inside this book will prove this to you – by doubling your reading speed... your power to learn any skill or subject and solve problems... your ability to completely out think others when you have to!

In this modern fast paced world of ours, your future success is going to depend on your ability to absorb facts, skills and procedures and put them to immediate use!

Let me repeat that – No matter what your age – whether you are a man or woman – self employed or working for a giant corporation – the entire quality of your life will be determined by your ability to learn, to think, to make your mind perform.

I mean that the size of your income, the station you attain in life, the kind of person who will choose you as his friend, even the satisfaction you get out of your spare time activities – all will be decided by your ability to keep up with thousands of men and women who are competing with you – and, if possible push ahead of them.

Does this sound exaggerated? Then consider these cold, hard facts:

1) About one-third of your entire adult life is spent at work. A man spends more time at his job than he does with his wife and family.

He earns his income from his job – gains his status from his job – makes most of his friends from his job.

2) And yet – from the very first day that you apply for that job – you are rated acceptable or rejectable on the basis of your ability to absorb facts, to master skills!

For example a college master's degree is worth $1.3 million more in lifetime earnings than a high school diploma, according to a recent report from the Commerce Department's Census Bureau. High school graduates can expect, on average, to earn $1.2 million; those with a bachelor's degree, $2.1 million; and people with a master's degree, $2.5 million.

Persons with doctoral degrees earn an average of $3.4 million during their working life, while those with professional degrees do best at $4.4 million.

3) But this is only the start of the overwhelming impact the ability to learn will have on your career! At every rung on the ladder – every time you're considered for a promotion or a new job – your ability to learn (and your ability to prove that learning in formal tests) will make the difference between skyrocketing up, or standing still!

Is It Really That Hard To Absorb Facts? The Answer Is No

Given average ability, men and women who have trouble learning in adult life do so because no one had ever taught them to study efficiently when they were children!

Without the proper study techniques, it is perfectly possible for you to understand only HALF what you should get of a newspaper, magazine, textbook, business letter or report! Without the proper retention techniques, it is possible for you to remember only HALF of what you have just read.

And without the proper techniques of filing and retaining that information you have stored away in your brain! We doom ourselves, through our negligence of the proper study techniques, to struggling through life as a HALF – DOER.

You do not have to be brilliant to succeed in life. The only thing separating the average man from a fruitful intellectual life is DIRECTION – the ability to get the best possible results out of your own efforts.

Given this direction, any man or woman with the average intelligence can learn new facts almost as quickly as he can read them. Every year, men and women who know how to study obtain business and social success far beyond that which might be expected from their IQ ability level. The difference is TECHNIQUE, pure and simple.

Technique... Direction... Guidance... Method!

These are the secrets of success in life. Not an IQ. Not "inborn ability". Not some mysterious hidden talent that enables a few gifted people to solve problems at a glance that other people would never be able to understand, no matter how hard they worked on them.

This idea is pure nonsense. The real difference between the top producer and the mediocre also – ran lies, not in ability, but in technique. And technique can be TAUGHT.

Because of this one simple fact – and because of the almost miraculous breakthroughs that have been achieved in the last few years in teaching people how to study – there is no longer any reason for any man or woman to be forever catching up while his friends are going forward, to suffer the gloom and discouragement of always being behind, to experience learning as drudgery and disappointment, to be branded as dull or slow minded.

Study is a skill, and it can be improved by practice like any other skill.

The ability to study can be improved drastically by learning a few simple techniques of studying scientifically.

And YOU can teach yourself enough of these techniques in a single week to literally start yourself on the road to doubling your power to learn.

Here Is Exactly What This Book Will Do For You

This is the purpose of this book. To teach you how to double your power to learn with the least effort, in the shortest possible time.

1. They will destroy present study habits that make learning unpleasant and burdensome, and replace them with new, simpler and easier habits that turn study into a thrilling, soaring hour of achievement every time you open a book.
2. In other words, they will reduce effective study procedures to the habit level. They will make them a part of your mind, so that you get right down to the core of every lesson, every report, every article – automatically, the instant you set your eyes on it.
3. Because of these new study habits, and sooner than you dare expect today, your ability to learn and to perform will zoom, will reveal such a change that your boss or friends may actually ask you what happened.

4. Self-improvement periods-learning periods will shrink in time- sometimes actually in half – while the work turned out from them will double in quantity and quality.
5. And there will be no more forcing yourself to learn. Learning will suddenly become a privilege rather than a punishment, because each new lesson will give you a new taste of success, a new thrill of understanding, a stronger and stronger realization that you can conquer knowledge and make it your own, day after day.

Isn't it worth 5 minutes of thrilling application every day while your forging ahead?

All the equipment you need is right here. These simple rules apply to any man or woman, with an average inborn intelligence, with any level of previous education.

To put them to work for YOU – to carve out the life of success and achievement you want for YOURSELF – you start right here.

PART ONE
The Simple Strategy Of Power Learning

CHAPTER 1
How good are your study habits today? Take this 3-minute test

Are you living up to your full potential? Are you squeezing out the absolute top achievement that your inborn intelligence will give you?

In other words, are your present learning habits helping or hindering you? Is the power of your brain being harnessed from the very first minute you open a book or blocked every step of the way?

This three-minute check list will tell you right now. It is a quick, scientific run-down, not of your intelligence or ability, but of the results your present learning habits are capable of giving you.

Simply observe your learning habits for a single night. Then answer these questions with a yes or a no. In three brief minutes, every weak spot in your learning pattern will be thrown into the spot-light.

You'll see the road-blocks in your way, and you'll take your first step toward removing them.

Here they are. Answer them coldly and honestly. DO YOU:

Find it hard to keep your mind on what you're reading? Have trouble picking out the main points of the book you're reading?

Forget the next day what you read the night before? Have trouble finding books, pencils, notes, reports you want to work with?

Take hours to get yourself going on the material you want to learn? Spend fruitless hours trying to figure out standard problems in business mathematics?

Make the same mistakes over and over again?

Have difficulty expressing your thoughts on paper?

Imitate other people's reports, memos and letters rather than create your own?

Forget new vocabulary words almost as fast as you learn them? Write letters that are a mess of illegible scribbles and torn-up pages?

Never finish work on time? Cram desperately for advancement tests? Become sick with fear before such tests?

How many questions did you answer with yes? If there was even one, this book will be worth far more to you than the price you paid for it.

If you had four yes answers, then you are losing over 25 per cent of your brain power through sloppy learning habits. In other words, you are achieving at least 25 per cent poorer grades than inborn ability should give you. This book will restore those lost percentage points.

And if you had eight or more yes answers, then you are in trouble; you can see it at a glance; and you are in for one of the most dramatic and painless improvement performances of your entire life.

Save this test. Check your answers, in pen or pencil, on this page. Refer back to each yes answer – to each weak point – as you reach the section that covers it in this book.

Then, one week from now, when you've finished this book, and you have run through the methods described in its pages – at that point take this test again. Write down your new answers - one week from today – next to the old.

The difference may actually take your breath away. You can actually see yourself grow, see your learning habits change in the first week, see yourself turn the corner to success.

And if there are any yes answers left at the end of that first week – then simply mark those weak points. Run over the procedures again. And repeat the test one month later.

You'll see those yes answers evaporate like water on a hot stove. And you'll see the results of those procedures – in black and white – on your next rating sheet – on the faces of your boss and friends – on the type of people you can now hold spell - bound with your conversation – on the type of book you can now read and repeat – on the new promotion you've earned – the raise you've deserved – the feeling of sheer simple satisfaction you've carved out for yourself – with your own mind!

CHAPTER 2
Our plan of attack for more learning power overnight – this is all you have to do!

In the past few years, a great many people have become confused. They have become so fascinated with social studies, physics, foreign languages, and the like, that they have forgotten how simple a good education really is.

A good education – a bedrock education – an education upon which you will either succeed or fail for the rest of your life – consists of just simple skills:

The ability to read, The ability to express thoughts in words, and The ability to solve mathematical problems.

THE THREE SIMPLE BUILDING BLOCKS OF SUCCESS

Reading, writing and arithmetic. The old-timers knew it. We've forgotten it; and we have to get back to it.

These are the foundation stones. Everything else, all the advanced subjects, depends on them. For example, if you can't understand what you read, you can't read science.

If you can't solve simple problems in addition or subtraction then you won't even be able to start on calculus or aerodynamics.

Everything you do in your business life, for example depends upon your ability to read, to write, and to figure. For the rest of your life, you'll be reading newspapers, memos, articles, and reports.

For the rest of your life, you'll be writing letters, applications, recommendations, and progress reports. For the rest of your life, you'll be figuring grocery bills, installment chargers, mortgage payments, and profit and loss.

If you can't read like an expert, write like an expert, and figure like an expert, then anything else you do for your mind will be wasted.

Therefore your fundamental task – the one great secret of building success into your life – is to make absolutely sure that you're a "blooming genius" in reading, writing and mathematics.

And I mean genius! When we get through with that mind of yours, we're going to have your friends pop-eyed at your ability to read a printed a page, to turn out a written report, to cut through a mathematical problem to its very heart.

Reading, writing, and mathematics. You are going to make yourself a master in each of these. And you are going to do it in five short minutes a day, using these three incredibly powerful tools:

Brand-new scientific techniques, Daily application And that wonderful feeling of accomplishment every time you master something new! Here's how they combine to get you off to a whiz-bang start – today.

WHAT YOU READ MEANS NOTHING. IT'S WHAT YOU CAN PUT TO USE THAT COUNTS

Your primary job, then, is twofold. First you must teach yourself the new scientific techniques of reading, writing, and mathematics contained in this book.

And second, you must put them to use every day, so you can make absolutely sure you've got them right.

This is the one-two punch that knocks tough subjects onto a cocked hat, that shoots learning power up overnight.

In computer language, this daily check-up process is called "feedback". Engineers know it's not what you feed into a computer that

counts; it's what that computer does with the information – what it "feeds back" to you – that counts.

Some of that information can be lost, forgotten, or distorted. You have to ask for it again to make sure.

The same with your own mind. In everything you learn, for every day of your life, what you read means nothing. Words can simply pour in and out of your mind like water through a funnel.

The only thing that counts is what sticks. How much you understand. How much you remember. And how much you can put to immediate use.

Burn this fact into your mind. To learn any subject, mere reading is only the first step. The complete, effective learning process is made up of these four steps:

Reading Understanding, Remembering, and Reproducing the key thoughts in your own words.

This is the end goal you want. Reproducing, putting to use, expressing in your own words, either on paper or in conversation with your friends. (Or, in the case of mathematics, in solving new problems.)

This is what you are aiming at, the end result. If your learning process stops short of this goal, this effective self expression, then you are getting only half the benefit of your work.

You have to make sure that you get it all. You have to apply these incredibly powerful new learning techniques every single day. Here's how you do it:

THE TEN-MINUTE ACHIEVEMENT CHECK ON THE MATERIAL YOU LEARN FROM THIS BOOK

Starting today, and continuing for every day that you read this book, do this:

Spend at least ten minutes a day putting these new ways of learning to work. The time of day is unimportant; but you must be able to give that time completely to your work, in full concentration upon these new methods, with no interruptions and no sense of being hurried.

For these few minutes each day, nothing in the world matters but your mind and the accomplishments it is giving you!

This will be the time you first read a magazine article in five minutes and startle your friends that very same night by rattling off every main point contained in it.

This will be the time you first open the door to a new field of knowledge you've always dreamed of mastering – psychology, law, engineering, computer programming – and find that you can flash through it – absorbing its facts and theories like a sponge.

14

Yes, this is the time when you just discover that you can put words on paper that sing – that grasp men's attention – that change their minds – that make them act in the paths and directions that you want them to act!

At the beginning, you will work no more than ten minutes a day. But then, as your skill grows greater and greater as you become more and more confident in your own ability to learn – you will want to devote more time each day to this thrilling new opportunity for self-expression and self-growth.

You will understand – perhaps for the first time in your life the true joy learning!

IN SUMMARY: Your entire education rests on your mastery of three bedrock skills:

Reading, Writing, Mathematics.

The purpose of this book is to help you improve those skills to the point of near perfection. This is done in two ways:

1. By teaching yourself new scientific techniques of learning how to learn and
2. By checking back on your growth every day, to make sure you have understood these techniques and put them to use.

Through this simple procedure, you will automatically learn a respect for, and a striving toward, that most magic of all words – excellence.

We are striving in this book for excellence. Nothing less will do.

And we begin by teaching you a few simple tricks of organization, to help you get twice as much done in half the time you spend today.

CHAPTER 3
Organization – How to get twice as much done in half the time

Most people waste at least half their reading and learning time, because no one has ever shown them how to organize their work.

This is the purpose of this chapter – to cut the waste out of your learning, and make sure you get a full minute's results for every minute you spend with your books.

WHAT IS ORGANIZATION?

Organization is simply planned direction. It is a procedure. A system. A planned schedule of events or tasks, one after the other, that gets something done in the shortest possible time, with the least amount of waste.

It is doing the right thing at the right time. And not wasting your time doing the wrong thing.

In regard to your learning growth, therefore, organization is basically a way of sitting down at a desk, finding out what has to be done, opening the right book to the right page., starting to do it at the beginning, learning it step by step, knowing when it is finished and when it is right, and then remembering what it is you have done, how you have done it, and what use you can put it to tomorrow.

Without such a definite step-by-step plan of attack, you waste much of your time. Because you will not get down to work immediately.

You will not be sure exactly what it is you are supposed to learn. You will wander aimlessly till you stumble on it. And then you may lose it again, waste time reading on after you have learned, or forget it before you get to use it the next day.

Therefore the most beautiful thing about organization is that it is far simpler and far easier than what you are doing today. It not only gives you far better understanding – instantly – but it does it with far less study time.

And it's so easy to put into practice. All the organization you need can be broken down into two simple formulas:

1. Getting down to work
2. Doing the work right.

Let's look at each of them in turn

NO MORE CRISES. NO MORE FEAR

Any subject you wish to learn becomes easy if you organize it on a long-term basis, day-by-day, lesson-by-lesson, step-by-step. Constant, daily study periods therefore are the fist magic key to success.

The first step in organizing your study habits is to set up a daily work schedule, and make sure you stick to it.

There is just no substitute for regular daily study – for a certain amount of time-spent daily on each subject. Learning – any kind of learning – becomes incredibly easy if you maintain a steady pace from start to finish.

Then there are no sudden pressures to get things done. No near – hysteria about deadlines No tensions and anxieties if you're going to take a test to earn a degree in that subject.

With a daily work schedule, religiously enforced, all these crises are miraculously replaced by the wonderfully secure feeling of being adequately prepared. Which in turn, leads to a steady, comforting flow of high marks towards that degree you may be seeking.

Let's look at such a daily schedule, and see how simple it is to set up, and how easy it is to follow.

YOUR DAILY ACHIEVEMENT SCHEDULE

Monday through Friday

7:00 A.M – Get up time
7:05 – 7:30 – Wash, dress, shine shoes
7:30 – 7:45 – Breakfast
7:45 – 8:00 – Help around the house
8:00 – 8:10 – Final preparation for work
8:10 – 8:30 – Going to work
8:30 – 8:45 – Pre-work talk with friends
8:45 – 12:45 – Regular work schedule
12:45 – 1:45 – Lunch
1:45 – 5:45 – Work
5:45 – 6:05 – Going home
6:05 – 7:00 – Dinner
 6:30 – 6:45 – Help with clean up
6:45 – 7:00 – Make ready for study time – get all equipment together
7:00 – 8:00 – Study hour (or half-hour, or whatever time you prefer)
8:00 – 11:00 – Watch TV, read, relax
11:00 – 11:15 – Prepare for bed
11:15 – 7:00 – Sleep
Saturday – a free day Sunday – a free day

The exact details in this schedule are, of course, merely suggestions. Your own family activities may dictate different dinner hours, relaxation breaks, and so on.

But the important points are clear. Every day - every single day – there should be a definite period for study and application of what you have learned. Without exception. Without excuse.

Without delay.

This study period is essential to your career. And it must start at exactly the same time each night. It must be entered into without delay. And it must be followed by a careful, concentrated check on what you've learned before you can close your books and go on to something else.

Let's take a closer look at that daily study period and see how we can make it produce twice the results for you.

TIPS THAT DOUBLE THE VALUE OF EACH STUDY HOUR

1. You will not do top work in your study period unless you make that study period as important to you as your work downtown. This means:
2. You must have a definite place to study. It must be the same place each night. With no one else having any claim to it for that hour.
3. It must be comfortable and bright. With the physical equipment you need to read and write permanently stored there, instantly at hand when you want to use it.
4. There must be no distractions for that hour. This means, ideally a room with door closed. No radio or TV. No interruptions. No friends working with you. No phone calls

permitted for any reason. When you get down to work, you stay at work till you're finished. This means no other members of the family with you. No conversations near by, no rustle of newspapers. You need silence to concentrate. And you have to make whatever sacrifices are necessary to give it to yourself.

5. But this ruling out of distractions goes one step further. It also means that you have with yourself, at study time, only equipment you need and nothing more. No unnecessary books. No newspapers. No pretty pictures on the wall to draw away your attention. Study is business all business.

6. Make sure you start your lessons at the same exact moment every day. A five-minute delay can kill an entire study period. The phone conversation is cut off, and you're at your desk at the precise moment you're scheduled to be there.

7. You are setting up a routine. A constant, daily psychological readiness to study. An automatic ability to concentrate that can only come from getting down to work at the same time, in the same spot, every day.

Once this routine is established, waste motion is eliminated and work flashes by. At the end of that period, when you are ready to review that work, you will be delighted at the quantity and quality of it.

IN SUMMARY: Organization is planned direction. It is your ability to:

1. Get down to work without waste motion,
2. Get the work done right

In this chapter we have seen that organization makes even the hardest subjects easy by attacking them on a day-after-day basis.

In order to do this, a definite study hour must be set aside every day, at exactly the same time, in exactly the same spot, with exactly the same equipment.

Once this routine is established, getting down to work becomes instant and automatic. You're ready to slash into your work without a second's waste motion.

Now let's go on to the second part of organization: How to fill up that study period with achievement. How to do that work right.

We'll start with the basic art of reading. How to cut through it in half your present time, with absolute understanding of every word you read.

Part TWO
Digging out the facts – reading

CHAPTER 4
How to become a master reader in three easy steps

The basic, fundamental skill required for all education is reading.

Your ability to learn effectively, to thoroughly understand any subject, depends almost entirely on your ability to read. On your ability to pull facts out of a printed page and make them your own.

Even in mathematics, you must first read the instructions and then understand precisely what you are to do to solve each of the problems.

If you cannot do this, if you cannot read any printed page that is handed to you with complete confidence and understanding, then you will go through crippling handicaps:

1. You will be forever doing unnecessary work. Every assignment will become doubly difficult – read over and over again two or more times, with each sentence painfully spelled out and only partially.
2. You will be forever making unnecessary mistakes. For example, professional educators acknowledge that almost as many errors are made in tests through sheer misreading or misunderstanding of instructions alone as through lack of knowledge.

Why burden yourself for the rest of your life with this double waste? Especially when effective reading – active, aggressive reading that tears knowledge out of the printed page and burns it into your memory for good – is far easier and far faster than the "spell-along" reading most people do today.

Here's why.

GOOD READING IS FAR MORE THAN MERELY RECOGNIZING WORDS

We will assume in this book that you already read normally. In other words, that you can take the letters c-a-t and put them together to form the word "cat". And that you can take several such words, and read them in the sentence, "The cat chases the mouse."

This, really, is what most people usually mean when they speak of the activity "reading." That you can mechanically scan a printed page and put the words together from that page to form sentences.

In turn, this mechanical reading, by some magic process, is supposed to put knowledge in your mind. According to this theory, once you have to read a sentence, or a series of sentences, the thought contained in them is supposed to automatically be transferred into your memory.

This is nonsense. Absolute nonsense. Everyone, at one time or another, has read an entire page, and then not been able to remember a single fact from it five minutes later.

Mere Mechanical reading is not enough. Passive reading is not enough. The ability to run your eye over a printed page – to make words out of words out of print on that page and put page – to make words out of print on that page and put them together into sentences – is only the beginning of Effective Reading.

Effective Reading is far more than this. Effective Reading goes one step beyond mere words. Effective Reading is the art of taking those words, and boiling them down into THOUGHTS. Of boiling down dozens, and even hundreds, of those words into ONE VITAL THOUGHT.

Of searching for the "guts" of an assignment – the two or three really important thoughts that it contains – and separating them from all the waste words and unnecessary details that surround them.

And then burning those few vital thoughts into your memory, so you can never forget them.

GOOD READING IS A SEARCH. A SEARCH FOR BIG IDEAS

Let me repeat these all-important facts. You must be trained, not merely to read for words, but for central thoughts.

You must be taught that good reading is an active, aggressive search that has three steps:

1. Locating a main idea in the mass of words that contain it.
2. Separating that idea from its unnecessary details. And
3. Boiling that idea down into a few easily remembered words.

You become a good reader, therefore, only when you master this technique of searching and boiling down. Searching and boiling down. Searching and boiling down.

Till you have taken the entire assignment – hundreds upon hundreds of words, sentences, and paragraphs – and reduced them to a few vital thoughts that contain the meaning of them all.

And that can be burned into your memory forever in a few short moments. Ready to be put to use – to solve new problems at business, or to answer questions in an examination – the very instant you need them.

THIS IS A NEW WAY TO READ. TWICE AS FAST. FIVE TIMES AS EFFECTIVE

The rest of this section will be developed to teaching you to read this new way. It is surprisingly easy to learn. And it is far easier, and far faster, than your present method.

Let me outline right now what each of the following chapters is going to teach you.

There are three easy steps to this new reading process. Each of the next three chapters explains one of them.

Chapter 5 shows you how to set up the search for big ideas. How to glance over your assignment, in one or two short minutes, and locate each of its important thoughts before you begin to read.

Chapter 6 shows you how to Power Read. How to flash through page after page, pulling out and marking down those important thoughts, merely glancing over their unnecessary details, and finishing with the assignment in half the time it has taken you before.

Chapter 7 show you how to boil these vital thoughts down into a few words, and burn them into your memory with the very same action.

Chapter 8 shows you how to use the same three step technique when you are listening to a lecture. It enables you to understand and remember what you hear as well as what you read.

When you have finished this section, and put its simple methods to use, you will be confident, accomplished reader. You will be able to read any book, any Article, any letter, any report that is given to you, easily, swiftly, and without fear. You will understand each word you read the instant you read it.

And you will remember the vital points of everything you read and be able to point them to immediate use.

IN SUMMARY:

Good reading is far more merely recognizing the meaning of words.

Good reading is an active, aggressive search for the major thoughts that are contained in these words.

This search has three steps:

1. Locating the main ideas.
2. Separating them from their unnecessary details. And
3. Boiling them down into a few words that can be easily memorized.

Now let's put these three steps into action. Let's examine each of these three steps into action. Let's examine each of these techniques in detail, along with concrete example of what they will accomplish for you.

CHAPTER 5
How to pre-read a lesson – understand it before you read

Let us suppose that you are given a reading assignment in a night school. For example, you are told to read Chapter 6 in history book on the Civil War. Or the next five pages in a book on Cost Accounting. Or perhaps even a complete book – let's say The Red Badge of Courage by Stephen Crane.

You take the book home. You sit down at your desk at the exact moment your evening study hour begins. And you open the book to the page assigned.

What do you do now?

If you simply begin to read the first words you see if you plunge right into that text without making any further preparation – then you are making a crucial mistake that will cost you hours of wasted effort every week, and that may cause you to miss the entire point of each lesson.

No one – no matter how bright – can you really understand an assignment by simply beginning to read it word after word. It's like trying to go on a car trip by simply driving on to the first motorway you see, without getting directions or looking at a map

Your job in reading is to get those directions. To build yourself that road map. To know exactly what you want to get out of that lesson. And where it's located.

To do this, you pre-read that lesson. You glance over that lesson from the beginning to end – before you start to read it. And you pick out the following information:

1. What's the main theme of this lessons? (For example the Civil War)
2. How much information does this lesson cover? (The period from 1861 to 1864)
3. What are the main thoughts in this lesson that I have to remember? (The crucial battle that turned the tide of the war)
4. How many of these main thoughts are there? (about five or six)
5. What do I have to remember about each one of these main thoughts? (The outcome of each battle)
6. Where in the lesson do I find this information? (Now you begin to read)

JUST LOOK AT THE DIFFERENCE THESE FEW QUESTIONS MAKE

Now, what exactly has happened here? You have invested one or two brief minutes to glance over your lesson from beginning to end. In that short time, you have picked out its main theme and each of its central thoughts. You have built a skeleton of that lesson – an outline of that lesson - a road map of that lesson to follow as you read.

Now you know what you are looking for. Now you are walking a lighted path instead of stumbling in the dark. Now, instead of facing a confused jumble words, you slash through that lesson with this definite purpose in mind:

What do I have to remember about each one of my main thoughts? (What was the outcome of each battle in this history lesson?)

Now you read to answer this question. You have direction. In one or two minutes, you have a better grasp of that assignment than if read it aimlessly for a full hour.

HOW YOU FIND THESE MAIN THOUGHTS: SIGN POSTS IN THE LESSON THAT POINT THEM RIGHT OUT TO YOU

Fortunately, the authors of your books agree with this road-map idea. They too believe that you should first build an outline of the important thoughts in each lesson, and then simply fill in the details.

In order to help you do this, they have built into their books certain signposts that point out these main thoughts. These signposts stick out from the main body of the text.

They are the chapter headings, section headings, table of contents, summary paragraphs, and other vital points set off by capital letters, underlining, italics, and other attention-drawings devices.

They form a book within a book. And by learning how to read them, you can pick out the main points of that book almost as fast as you can turn its pages.

Let's see how to really use them, right now. Let's start with big signposts, the ones that will give you the guts of that entire book in five to ten minutes.

And then let's work our way down to the smaller signposts, the ones that will organize your learning each time you read another chapter in that book.

For our first few chapters, we'll use this book – the one you're reading now. This will give you a chance to check your present reading habits, to see if you're getting as much information out of each page as you should.

Then we'll go on to examples from standard textbooks. And then we'll see how the same simple techniques apply to everything you read – letting you pull information out of newspapers, magazines, and so on, almost as fast as you can run your eyes down their pages.

Here we go!

SIGNPOST PARTS OF EVERY BOOK AND WHAT EACH ONE TELLS YOU

1. THE TITLE What it tells you: Actually, a good title should give you, in a single phrase, the main theme of the book. What it is about, and what it is not about. It is your first concrete information about what you are to learn in the pages that follow. Make sure you understand it before you read on.

Example: The title of the book is The 5 Minute Learning Machine. This title contains two separate pieces of information. First, the subject, which is your ability to learn. Second, a specific goal – 5 minutes.

Starting from this title, and knowing exactly what you should get out of this book, you read on with one purpose – to answer the question "how?"

How do I become a 5 minute learning machine? To answer this question, you turn to the next big signpost part of the book:

2. THE TABLE OF CONTENTS What it tells you: The table of contents takes the grand plan, the ultimate goal you are shooting for, and breaks it down into a step-by-step process. It shows you the steps you have to take, one after another, to attain that goal.

This table of contents is actually a ready made outline of the book that should be studied carefully before you read one word of text. By carefully going over this table of contents, you immediately gain an over-all picture of the skeleton of the book.

You see the relationships between each of the various chapters and the main theme of the book. You know exactly where you are going when you start to read – to such a degree that you can even set up a time schedule of so many days per chapter to finish the book when you have to.

For example: In this book, the table of contents is broken down into six main parts, and then into twenty-four chapters. Let's start with the main parts first, and see how they give us the over-all plan of the book at a glance. Here they are:

The Simple Strategy Of Power Learning. (What we are going to do how we are going to do it.) Digging Out the Facts – Reading. Expressing the Facts – Writing and Conversing.

Mathematics Can Be Fun, If You Do It This Way. Mastering Facts – The Art of Remembering and Review. How to Breeze Through Tests.

By simply glancing at these six titles, you immediately see that the book is going to concentrate on reading, writing, and mathematics to the extent of devoting full sections to each of them. Then it's going to show you how to review for any test you may encounter, and make top grades in them.

Thus the general goal of being a 5 minute learning machine (becoming learning machine in only 5 minutes a day) , which was promised in the title, has now been broken down into specific, step-by-step goals of improving your reading, writing, and ability to solve problems, helping you over problem areas, and sharpening your ability to take tests.

Now the table of contents goes on to show us more concretely how we're going to accomplish each one of these major goals. It does this by listing the chapter headings under each of them. For example, in the next part of this book, on writing, we find these two chapters:

Correct Spelling Made Easy. How to Write as Easily and Quickly As You Think.

Now you can see that there are only two steps to improve your writing. First, spelling; then the actual construction of sentences and paragraphs.

Again we see the grand plan of the book developing before your eyes. From the over-all goal becoming a learning machine in only 5 minutes a day, we have gone on to the six major steps for doing this, and then we have taken one of those steps, which is writing, and learned two separate ways in which it alone can be improved.

We can do the same thing for each of the other four major parts of the book. Each major part of the book has its own chapter headings underneath it, which shows you step by step how you are going to achieve it.

You have now finished reading the title and the table of contents. You have spent perhaps five minutes on the book so far. And yet know:

1. What it is going to do for you, and
2. How it is going to do it, perfectly

From this point on, you will read simply to answer the questions each one of these chapter headings has raised in your mind. For example, going back to section on writing again:

How do I spell a word correctly when I have misspelled it every time before now?

What are the techniques that allow me to write easily and quickly?

At this point you could open to the first page of text, and read faster and with much greater understanding than you have ever read before. But, before you do this, there are two other big signposts you will want to check, to help you get every ounce of information out of the book.

3. The INDEX   What it tells you: The index is a storehouse of minor topics of special interest to you. There they are alphabetically arranged for instant reference.

For example: Glance at the index of this book. Pick out a topic of special interest to you, or a problem that you are facing today. For instance, take problem-solving. Look up problem-solving in the index.

Turn to the pages indicated there. And glance at, do not read, the treatment given to them.

Instantly you can see the concrete, step-by-step methods that make those problems easy. There's no need to read them, word by word, now, since you'll get up to them later this week. And in the proper time and place in the book, they'll means far more to you.

But now you know that they're there, and that they're complete. And if you ever have to refer back to them after you finish the book, the index will tell you where they're located at a glance. And now we turn to the last of our big signposts:

4. THE INTRODUCTION, OR PREFACE, OR FOREWORD.

What it tells you: This is the author's personal message to you, before he gets down to the body of the book. In it, he may

Explain why he chose this particular title, Or tell you what compelled him to write the book, Or show you in advance what he is trying to accomplish, Or give you a brief, one or two paragraph condensation of its contents, Or list the main sources from which he got his information, Or list the main reason why this book should be important to you, Or in any other way give you a brief outlining of where you will be heading in the book and what benefits it will give you.

It is the personal note, the personal touch that rounds out your quick survey of the book and give you insight into the author himself and his purpose in writing the book, as well as its contents.

For example: The introduction in this book is divided into three distinct parts, each of which serves a very definite purpose.

Part 1 of the introduction points out the overwhelming importance of learning power to your future, and lists ten reasons why it is so vital.

Part 2 shows you that this door opening ability to absorb and use facts is really not that hard to develop and, once you learn the right technique, is actually well within the reach of any man or women of average or better ability.

The introduction to this book, therefore, is an attempt to encourage you with these three facts: that the goal you bought this book to attain is worth while, that it is obtainable, and that it will give you the results you wish.

When you have finished this introduction, you know exactly what goals you are out to get. Then, reading on through the table of contents, you realize, step by step, exactly how you are going to get them.

In your one brief survey of this book, or any other, you now know exactly what it is you want to get out of it, and where it is located. You are now ready to read the text itself. To cut through it to the heart off its main ideas, and do it almost as fast as your eyes can move down the page.

Let's now turn to the individual chapters, and see how this same exact method – looking for signposts first – can again mine their information for you at as single glance.

IN SUMMARY:

No matter how bright you may be, you cannot understand your assignments simply by reading them word by word.

Instead, you must first pre-read those assignments make a quick survey of them before your read to uncover their main thoughts. You do this, not only with each chapter you are assigned, but with each new book that you study. You find the main ideas of each of these books by checking the following four signpost parts of every book:

1. The title
2. The table of contents
3. The index
4. The introduction or preface

When you lift these signpost parts out of the text and arrange them in order, you will have at your fingertips an outline of the main thoughts of the entire book.

You can then read each individual chapter in order, with perfect understanding of how it ties into the chapter that has gone before it, the chapter that follows it, and the main theme of the book as a whole.

Now let's see how easy it is to pull out the main thoughts of each chapter in the same exact way.

CHAPTER 6
Signpost parts of every chapter, and what each one tells you

In the section above, when we looked at the four big signposts in every book – the title, the table of contents, the index, and the introduction – we used this book as our example.

This technique is used every time you open a new book. Using this technique, you get a bird's-eye view of the entire book, the first day you begin it. During the rest of the book, chapter by chapter, you are merely filling in important details, deepening your understanding of the grand plan you discovered in your first survey of the book.

To do this, apply to each individual chapter the same quick-survey you used at the beginning of the book. To illustrate this technique in action, let's turn now to three fresh examples – to typical textbooks you will meet in your work.

And let us see exactly what you should do to them, step by step. How much material you have left – and how much you have discarded – when you have finished reducing them to their main thoughts. And how you burn that material into your memory, for good.

Here are these examples, first reproduced word for word (I suggest you simply glance over them briefly now):

CHAPTER FROM A TEXTBOOK ON ENGLISH the four kinds of sentences

A declarative sentence makes a statement. It is followed by a period. EXAMPLE: Arthur is an accountant

An interrogative sentence asks something. It is a question. It is followed by a question mark. EXAMPLE: Do you have an accountant working for you?

To find the subject of an interrogative sentence, simply turn it into a declarative sentence. EXAMPLE: You do have an accountant working for you.

An Exclamatory sentence shows surprise or excitement. It is followed by an exclamation point. EXAMPLE: What a thrilling thought!

Sometimes an exclamatory sentence has to be changed to a simple declarative sentence before it is clear what the subject and predicate are. EXAMPLE:

A. Exclamatory: How Dick and John hate each other! B. The same sentence into a declarative sentence: Dick and John hate each other, how.

An imperative sentence gives a command. It is followed by either a period or an exclamation point. EXAMPLE: Tell me where you were!

In an imperative sentence the word you is always understood to be the subject. Example: (You) tell me where you were!

FIRST SECTION FROM A CHAPTER IN A TEXTBOOK ON WORLD HISTORY:

(I have numbered each paragraph at the end.) The Greeks

1. The Background

The ancient Greeks developed the first government that might be called democratic and the first great civilization to take permanent root on the mainland of Europe. Yet the Greek civilization that matured almost twenty-five hundred years ago was by no means purely European in character.

The Greeks inhabited the western coast of Asia Minor and the islands dotting the Aegean Sea as well as the European peninsula we call Greece. They also inherited some of the legacy of the older Near Eastern Civilizations, probably passed on to them through the Aegean civilization. (1)

Aegean Civilization

Aegean Civilization, which lasted for some two thousand years down to about 1100 B.C, apparently centered on the island of Crete at the southern entrance to the Aegean Sea. Crete had many natural advantages. Its mild climate favored agriculture; the sea give it some protection against invasion and conquest and at the same time promoted seafaring.

Located at the cross-roads of the Eastern Mediterranean, Crete was close enough to Asia, Africa and Europe for daring seaman to sail their primitive vessels to Egypt and Greece. Its geographical position doubtless made trade and piracy the natural occupations of the islanders. (2)

When copper and the manufacture of bronze were introduced, probably from Phoenicia or elsewhere in Asia Minor at some time before 3000 B.C, civilization began on Crete. The civilization is termed Minoan, from Minos, a legendary king, and archaeologists have divided it into three main chronological (3) :

Early Minoan – down to 2300 B.C Middle Minoan – 2300 to 1600 B.C Late Minoan – 1600 to 100 B.C (4)

Each of these main periods is subdivided into three segments, from I to III. The greatest flowering of culture on Crete seems to have occurred during the Middle Minoan III and the late Minoan I and II, between 1700 and 1400 B.C (5)

We must say "seems to have occurred," for our knowledge of ancient Crete is still incomplete. Up to the beginning of the twentieth century it was so sketchy that no methodical approach to its civilization was possible.

Then, in 1900, the British archaeologist, Sir Arthur Evans, acting on the well-founded hunch, began excavations at Cnossus in central Crete, a few miles inland from north shore of the island. He struck "pay-dirt" almost at once and started to uncover what was evidently a very large and very ancient palace, which he termed the "palace of Minos." Subsequent diggings by Evans and others disclosed the sites of more than hundred towns that had existed before 1500 B.C, a good amount of pottery, and stretches of paved road. (6)

More recently, hundreds of tablets with Aegean writing have also come to light, both in Crete itself and on the Greek mainland. Although no Minoan equivalent of the Rosetta stone has been found, one scholar announced in 1953 that by using the techniques of cryptography, he had begun the work of deciphering the tablets.

This discovery may eventually revolutionize our knowledge of Crete. Meanwhile, we have very little sure information on

Minoan politics, though it is conjectured that Crete, like Egypt, had despotic priest-kings who ruled with the aid of a central bureaucracy. (7)

The archaeological remains, however, provide convincing evidence that the Minoans were great builders, engineers and artists. The Palace at Cnossus was at least two stories high and filled an area equivalent to a city block. A city in miniature, it had running water, a sewage system, and a kind of playground used for dancing, wrestling and other sports.

The palace was begun in the Middle Minoan I period and was often repaired and altered, particularly after Middle Minoan II after a destructive earthquake. As a result, the excavated palace is a maze of storerooms, courtyards, corridors, workshops, living quarters and government offices. Sir Arthur Evans realized that he had very likely discovered the actual building that had inspired the Greek legend of the labyrinth to which the early Greeks were forced to send sacrificial victims. (8)

The skilled craftsmen of Crete apparently copied Egyptian techniques. They did marvelous work, from huge jars, as high as a man, to delicate little cups, no thicker than a eggshell, decorated with birds, flowers fishes and other natural designs. Painters executed large frescos of kings and warriors on the palace walls. Ivory, gold and jewels were used for the inlaid gaming boards of the kings and for exquisite statuettes, less than a foot high, of the bare-breasted snake-goddess, who was apparently one of the chief objects of worship. (9)

Crete at the height of its power may have controlled an empire including the other Aegean islands and, perhaps, the Aegean shores of Asia Minor and Greece. The recent work on Aegean tablets, of however, suggests that Crete itself may have become an outpost of the Greek mainland rather early. The extent of

Minoan political influence, which very likely reached to other parts of the Aegean world. (10)

A nineteenth-century German, Heinrich Schliemann, undertook excavations at Troy, in northwest Asia Minor, the scene of homer's Iliad, and at Mycenae on the Greek mainland, the home of Agamemnon, the leader of the Greek forces in the Trojan War of Homer's epic. Schliemann's determination resulted in a great archaeological romance - early poverty, business success in America, mastery of the Greek language, marriage to a Greek lady (she could recite Homer from memory!), and finally, later in life, discovery of the site of troy, though it turned that what he uncovered was a later city built on the ruins of Homeric Troy. (11)

Thanks to Schliemann and later experts, we now know that by 1400 B.C Troy and a group of cities centered a Mycenae in Greece had attained a degree of civilization strikingly similar to what had apparently been reached in Crete centuries earlier. Mycenaean pottery, though made of different materials, is similar to Minoan in design and ornamentation. At Mycenae, the kings were buried in large underground tombs, shaped like beehives, which resembled tombs built earlier in Crete. The cities on the mainland, however, built much more elaborate fortifications than did those of Crete. (12)

By about 1600 B.C, sporadic groups of invaders were filtering down from the north. They appear to have been Greeks, a people who spoke a language probably much like the classic Greek. The first Greeks seemed to have mixed rather peaceably with the existing populations of Greece, the Aegean islands, and Asia Minor, and to have acquired the Aegean culture that flourished at Mycenae and elsewhere. Later Greek invaders were more warlike and destructive. As tribe after tribe pushed south, the old Aegean civilization grew steadily weaker until it finally perished about 1100 B.C. By that time, the Greeks controlled the entire Aegean area, including Crete itself. (13)

The Setting of Greek Civilization

The forces of nature played a large part in shaping Greek civilization. The climate and geography of the Greek homeland have changed little since ancient times. As in the Mediterranean area as a whole, the rains come mainly between September and May. The summers are long, sunny and dry, but because of the sea breezes they are not intolerably hot.

People can live outdoors during the greater part of the year, and they can grow olives and other semi-tropical fruit. The sharply indented coastline and the profusion of mountains make a magnificent natural setting Nature

Combines such lavish amounts of sunshine and scenery only in California and a few other parts of the world. (14)

Greece, however has never had the immense fertile acres typical of California. The quality of the soil is poor, and the valleys and plains, squeezed by mountains are on a miniature scale. The rivers and streams are too swift and shallow for navigation; they flood in the rainy season, then dwindle to a trickle or dry up altogether. Local springs can supply the minimum needs of the population during the dry season, but they are not adequate for extensive irrigation. (15)

Greece, in short, has never afforded men an easy living, though it has often provided a reasonably pleasant one. The farms and orchards of ancient Greece produced barley and other grains, fruit, wine, honey and little else. Meat was a rarity. (16)

The Greek homeland, however, had one great geographical advantage: its situation encouraged navigation, even by the rather timid. The irregular coasts of the mainland and the islands provided sheltered anchorages; destructive storms seldom occurred during the long summer, the great season of navigation; and the vessels could go for hundreds of miles without ever losing sight of land.

Travel in ships propelled by sails or oars or a combination of the two was cheaper, swifter and more comfortable than an up-hill and down-dale journey over land. The Greeks, consequently, built up an active maritime trade. (17)

The geography of Greece favored political decentralization. In the valleys of the Tigris, the Euphrates and the Nile, the absence of natural barriers to travel had helped the building of large empires. In Greece, on the other hand, the frequent mountains and countless bays and gulfs impeded land communication. The individual valleys and plains, both on the mainland and on the islands, were natural geographic and economic units; they served as separate political units, too. (18)

The political unit was the polis or city-state, which included a city and the surrounding countryside. Most of the city-states were exceedingly limited in area; Greece, although a small country, contained many dozens of them. By modern standards, the average Greek city was at best a mere town, and many of its inhabitants were primarily farmers. A strong point, which could be readily defended against attack, was the nucleus of the city.

A familiar example is the Acropolis at Athens, with its commanding height its steep and difficult approaches. (19)

FROM A TEXTBOOK ON BUSINESS ADMINISTATION (I have numbered each paragraph at the end) Chapter2: Five Roads To Cost Reduction

Every management is faced with a continuing need to effect cost reduction. Somehow or other we think of these reductions

46

as available principally in the manufacturing process, but this is not the sole area for expense reduction. There are at least five channels through which important savings can be effected. These are (1):

1. Raw materials.   2. The costs of capital equipment 3. Manufacturing costs   4. Sales expense   5. General and administrative overhead expense (including the office). (2)

Although there are some procedures in common which you can use in endeavoring to reduce expenses along these five avenues, for the most part the approaches must be different. (3)

Road 1: Raw Materials

Raw materials costs vary greatly with industries. Most companies have long since worked out the average percentage of the sales dollar paid for raw materials and supplies. If you can make a comparison of this percentage for your company against other companies in your industry, you may have an excellent starting point. And even where you can't do this, or the comparison is favorable to your company, it nevertheless may pay you to study the ways of lowering the cost of raw materials. Here are the principal devices which companies have used (4):

1. Development of carefully prepared purchasing specifications, which demand raw material which is good enough for your manufacturing process but not of such high quality that your costs go up without a compensating increase in the price of your ultimate product. (5)
2. Inspection of incoming materials to make certain that they meet these specifications. (6)
3. Tracing back difficulties in the manufacturing process to raw materials imperfections. (7)
4. Modifications of manufacturing processes to eliminate the necessity for certain raw materials and supplies. (8)

5. Substitution of other kinds of raw materials. (9)
6. Control over the sources of raw materials either by purchase of supply sources (vertical integration) or by long term contractual arrangements. (10) Road 2: The Costs of Capital Equipment Filed upon manufacturing costs and material costs must be cost of capital equipment used. Typical of such costs would be depreciation, replacement, maintenance and interest on borrowed capital. (11)

A great many companies tie up a lot of money in semi finished or finished inventories. It's useful to make an occasional check as to the amount so tied up and compare it with previous checks. (12)

Because of inventory pricing policies used by accountants at the close of the year, many a company goes through the year thinking it has had a profitable operation, only to discover that the inventory pricing has sharply reduced the expected profit. (13)

In chapter 4 we shall consider capital financing in more detail, so we shall not make further comment here. (

Road 3: Manufacturing Costs

Manufacturing costs normally consist of labour plus material plus manufacturing overhead. (15)

Labour opens up a large area for study. It includes proper original selection, adequate training of workers, incentives, supervision, standards and control. It may involve aptitude testing, skill training, time and motion study, work simplification, etc. (16)

Reduction of manufacturing overhead may involve studies of supervision, maintenance and other indirect labour; of inspection and quality control; of fuel, light and power; of fire, safety and insurance protection; of idle equipment charges; of proper utilization of the space available; etc. (17)

Design for new equipment for production involves consideration of manufacturing methods and the capital investment required. (18)

Proper lighting has been responsible for worthwhile increases in productivity and reduction of accidents. Improvements have also resulted from painting of walls and machines, reduction in noise, better ventilation, etc. (19)

Materials handling is usually another fertile field for investigation. The movement and storage of raw materials, work in progress and finished goods can add considerably to the final cost of manufactured goods. (20)

Studies of productive operation may readily include operations research, whereby mathematics is applied to determine the optimum or best manufacturing conditions. Typical would be job lot size to derive the greatest advantage from manufacturing operations; proper inventories of raw materials, partial assemblies, semi-finished products and finished products. (21)

Road 4: Sales Expense

Over the present century there has been a reversal of the relationship of manufacturing costs to marketing costs. At one time manufacturing costs represent more than half the sales price of an article, but these costs have relatively receded so that today, in most companies, the sales costs represent more than half the sales price. Contributing to this increase in sales costs have been such items as warehousing, transportation, advertising, packaging, direct sales costs, and the constant price attrition of competition. Sales overhead, too, has increased through the addition of market research, sales promotion specialists, automatic vending equipment, more sales supervision. (22)

Road 5: General and Administrative Expense

The fifth avenue of cost reduction consists of analysis of general and administrative expense. In the normal company these cover such items as salaries of executives and office employees, office expense, interest, property depreciation, taxes, insurance, donations, legal fees, consultants, investigation of possible mergers, economic services and other general business expenses. (24)

IN SUMMARY:

The five roads to cost reduction are:

1. Raw materials
2. The costs of capital equipment
3. Manufacturing costs.
4. Sales Expenses
5. General and administrative expense. (26)

Once possible economies have been uncovered it is necessary to prosecute them vigorously, lest they fail of accomplishment through inertia and resistance to change. (27)

NOW LET'S GET TO WORK ON THOSE CHAPTERS. HERE'S HOW THE CHAPTER SIGNPOSTS BREAK THEM DOWN FOR YOU, IN MINUTES.

As you could tell at a glance, it's simply not enough for you to just read these sample chapters, word by word, from start to finish. If you try to do this, you will confuse detail with main idea, and you will remember almost nothing when you are through reading.

What you need is a key – a system – that will unlock that mass of words and pull out the main ideas for you.

This key is PRE-READING. The ability to read chapter signposts at a glance, and use them to pinpoint the main ideas of the chapter, one after the other, and give purpose and direction to your reading.

There are eight signposts parts of every chapter that you should know as well your own name. Let's review them one by one, and see how they pull the main ideas right out of these chapters before you begin to read the text.

1. THE CHAPTER TITLE

What it tells you: What the chapter is about. What it includes and does not include.

Examples: In the first chapter, the title The Four Kinds of Sentences show you that there are a specific number of definitions to learn – four. And each of these definitions describes a different kind of sentence. Thus

you know immediately what you are looking for – definitions – and how many you must find – four.

The third sample chapter gives the same information in its title. Five Roads to Cost Reduction tells you that you must find a specific number of ways to reduce costs – five – and must discover how and in what ways each one works.

The title of the second chapter: THE GREEKS, I. The Background is more vague. It does not tell how many parts you are to follow. But it does tell you that you are going to study Greeks, and what you are going to look for in the first section of the chapter is the effect of their background upon them. You must now read on, to the next chapter signposts, to discover what you must find out about their background. To do this, you turn to:

2. THE SECTION HEADINGS

What they tell you: The section headings break down the over-all chapter heading into its main parts. They list the names and number of important subjects to be covered in the chapter. Reading them quickly, without the intervening text, gives you the skeleton of the chapter.

Examples: The section headings in our third sample chapter read as follows:

Road 1: Raw Materials
Road 2: The Costs of Capital Equipment
Road 3: Manufacturing Costs
Road 4: Sales Expense
Road 5: General and Administrative Expense

Here are the five roads to cost reduction mentioned in the chapter title, laid out for you at a glance. You now know the entire structure of the chapter. Your only task now is to read the text, and find out how you can reduce costs in each of these areas.

In sample Chapter 2, however, the section headings are fewer in number and more vague. They are:

Aegean Civilization, and The Setting of Greek Civilization

These give you the two main sources of the background of Greek civilization. But they do not yet give you enough information on what you are to find out about each. Therefore you must go on to further signposts, which we will describe in a moment.

And in our first sample chapter, there are no section headings at all. So you check the next chapter signpost, which is:

3. PARAGRAPH HEADS OR BOLD PRINTS

What they tell you: The main topic of each paragraph. What the paragraph contains, boiled down into a single phrase.

For example: In this first sample chapter, the author has carefully stated the name of each kind of sentence. Listing them in order, we have:

Declarative sentence Interrogative sentence Exclamatory sentence Imperative sentence

Immediately, you know the names of the four kinds of sentences you are to learn in this lesson. Now all you have to do is read the text, and find out a definition for each of them.

In the other two sample chapters, there are no paragraph headings. And so we turn to the next chapter signpost:

4. INTRODUCTION PARAGRAPHS

What they tell you: Here the author points out what to look for in the text that follows. He gives an introduction to the chapter, ties it into the chapters that came before it, and reveals the main thought or thoughts in the material in the remainder of the chapter.

For example: In the second sample chapter, the author begins with this introductory paragraph (for the purposes of this survey, let's break the paragraph apart, point out each of its main thoughts, and state the purpose):

"The ancient Greeks developed the first government that might be called democratic and the first civilization to take permanent root on the mainland of Europe."

(This is the introduction to the chapter, pointing out the importance of the Greeks to us all.)

"Yet the Greek civilization that matured almost twenty five hundred years ago was by no means purely European in character."

(Now the authors lead us from the introductory sentence to the non- European background of the Greeks. This is what they are going to discuss in the material that follows.)

"The Greeks inhabited the western coast of Asia Minor and the islands dotting the Aegean Sea as well as the European peninsula we call Greece."

(We are told the first important influence, the geographical setting.)

"They also inherited some of the legacy of the older Near Eastern civilizations, probably passed on to them through the Aegean Civilization."

(And now we are told the second vital influence, the Aegean civilization.)

Thus the introductory paragraph confirms the two main divisions in the chapter – the Aegean Civilization and the Geographical Setting – that were revealed earlier by a survey of the section headings. Now you know you're on the right track. But you're looking for further subdivisions. So you continue to search to the next chapter signpost.

Usually you would next check:

5. THE SUMMARY OR CLOSING PARAGRAPHS

What they tell you: The summary paragraphs are the author's last words on the chapter. They are his own outline of the material he has covered in this chapter before he passes on to the next. They are a declaration of what he deems important out of all the material you have just read.

Sometimes he sums this material up in one paragraph. Sometimes he outlines each idea in a separate phrase, paragraphs it, and may even number it. Sometimes he rephrases the important points in the form of questions.

In any case, these final words deserve careful study before you begin the text.

For example: Since there is no summary paragraph in our second sample chapter, let's use the one in the third chapter as our example. It reads:

"In Summary: The five roads to cost reduction are:

1. Raw Materials
2. The Costs of Capital Equipment
3. Manufacturing Costs
4. Sales Expense
5. General and Administrative Expense

Once possible economies have been uncovered, it is necessary to prosecute them vigorously, lest they fail of accomplishment through inertia and resistance to change."

These sentences confirm what you have already discovered. You are now doubly sure that you have the five roads to cost reduction firmly outlined in your mind; and, especially on the basis of the last paragraph in the summary, now you only have to read on to discover how you can reduce costs in each of these areas.

You now turn to the next chapter signpost:

6. THE FIRST SENTENCE OF EACH PARAGRAPH

What they tell you: As you remember, this Pre-Reading, this quick survey of an entire chapter before you begin the text, is essentially a search. A search for the main thoughts of the chapter – for a quick outline of that chapter that tells you exactly what you are looking for and where to find it.

This search begins with the chapter title, and continues one by one, with each of the following chapter signposts till you have uncovered those main ideas-till you have built your outline.

At this point, when you have located the main ideas in the chapter, you stop the Pre-Reading and begin the text. The Pre-Reading is a search for the chapter's main ideas. When you have found them, you begin to read.

Therefore you do not check all the chapter signposts in each Pre-Reading of each chapter. You check only enough signposts to give you your main ideas, and then ignore the others.

For example, in the first sample chapter, you needed only to read the chapter title, then check to see that there were no section headings, and then simply pick up your main ideas out of underlined paragraph headings. At that point, you had the four kinds of sentences, and would immediately begin to read the text to find a definition for each.

However, it is the second sample chapter that forces you to make a deeper survey. In this second chapter, you have read title, found only two section headings, found no paragraph heads, discovered that the introductory paragraph merely confirms and two main ideas you learned from the section headings, and again found that there was no summary paragraph.

So what you have gained from your first five signposts is this. You know that you are to learn about the background of Greek civilization. And you know that there are two sources of this background – the Aegean civilization, and the geographical setting of Greece.

What you still do not know, however, is what each of these sources contributed to Greek civilization. You have to uncover these contributions – how many there were and what each of them was – before you can begin reading with definite clear-cut goals in mind.

Therefore, you probe deeper. You turn to the next chapter signpost – the first sentence of each paragraph.

In most cases, especially if the author has done his work well, these first sentences are called topic sentences. They give the main idea of the paragraph, and let the remaining sentences fill in the details.

So, if you take the first sentence of each paragraph and string them together, you should have a fairly good outline of the mina ideas in the chapter.

Unfortunately, this method is not as automatic or as clear cut as those using the first five signposts. You have to use more judgment in weeding out paragraphs that don't really contain main ideas.

But in those rare cases when the first five signposts don't do this job, you must go on with the sixth. Let's see how this method opens up the main ideas in this massive second chapter:

For example: The first sentences of each paragraph in the second chapter are these. (We will give each sentence the number of the paragraph it comes from. And we will leave out the first introductory sentence, since we have already covered it):

"AEGEAN CIVILIZATION

1. Aegean civilization, which lasted for some two thousand years down to about 1100B.C., apparently centered on the island of Crete at the southern entrance to the Aegean Sea.
2. When the copper and the manufacture of bronze were introduced, probably from Phoenicia or elsewhere in Asia Minor at some time before 3000 B.C., civilization begun on Crete
3. (Unimportant)
4. (Unimportant)
5. (Unimportant)
6. (Unimportant)
7. The archaeological remains, however, provide convincing evidence that the Minoans were great builders, engineers and artists.
8. (Unimportant)

9. Crete at the height of its power may have controlled an empire including the other Aegean islands and, perhaps, the Aegean shores of Asia Minor and Greece.
10. (Unimportant)
11. Thanks to Schliemann and later experts, we now know that by 1400 B.C. Troy and a group of cities centered at Mycenae in Greece had attained a degree of civilization strikingly similar to what had apparently been reached in Crete centuries earlier.
12. (Unimportant)
13. The forces of nature played a large part in shaping Greek civilization
14. (Unimportant)
15. (Unimportant)
16. The Greek homeland, however, had one great geographical advantage: its situation encouraged navigation, even by the very timid.
17. The geography of Greece favored political decentralization/
18. (Unimportant)"

These are the first sentences of each important paragraph in the chapter. Already, in choosing them, the boiling-down process has begun. Already unnecessary words and details have been thrown away. You are looking only for main ideas. You therefore choose only those paragraphs that contain those main ideas.

But how do you know which paragraph to choose and which leave out? In a very simple way.

You already know the main theme of the chapter, THE GREEKS, 1. The background, which was given to you in the chapter title.

You already know the two main sources of the back-ground, Aegean Civilization and the Geographical Setting, which were given to you in the section headings.

You do not know, however, how many divisions each of these two sources have, and what each contributed to Greek civilization. This is the information you are looking for in the first sentence of each paragraph.

And you are looking only for big contributions, not details.

Therefore you will judge each sentence by these two simple rules:

1. They must talk about the main theme of the chapter, and not about some side issue.

In this case, they must talk about the Aegean contribution to the background of Greek civilization, or about the geographical contribution to that background, and about nothing else.

2. They must bring in a new main point, and not merely furnish details about a main point brought up by the paragraph before.

These are the two rules of what to leave in and what to throw out. They are quite simple to follow. Let's see how they eliminate most of the paragraphs in this second sample chapter, and leave only the main points.

Sentence 2: Mentions Crete as the centre of Aegean civilization. Leave it in.

Sentence 3: Shows high civilization, based on metals, that Crete contributed to Greeks. Leave it in.

Sentence 4: Just dates of Minoan culture. No contribution to Greeks. Throw it out.

Sentence 5: More Minoan periods. Out

Sentence 6: Says nothing but that our knowledge of Crete is incomplete. No contribution here. Probably a side issue. Throw it out.

Sentence 7: Another scientific side issue. Out.

Sentence 8: Now we get to basic contributions from the Minoans – buildings, engineering, artistry. Leave it in.

Sentence 9: Details about Minoan art. We already have art in the sentence above. Leave it out.

Sentence 10: Discuss Minoan seafaring, politics, war – all picked up by Greeks later on. Leave it in.

Sentence 11: Side issue. Interesting but not important

Sentence 12: Identifies other centres of Aegean civilization. Now we know there were two – Crete and Mycenae. And we know that they both made essentially the same contributions. A good find. Leave it in.

Sentence 13: Talks about invaders, not Aegean's. Not on topic we want. Throw it out.

Sentence 14: Identifies forces of nature as first great geographical influence of Greeks. Leave it in.

Sentence 15: Detail under natural forces (soil conditions) Leave it out.

Sentence 16: Mere comment on effect of natural forces. Covered already by sentence 14 above. Out

Sentence 17: New effect of geographical setting – navigation water. Important. Leave it in.

Sentence 18: A third main effect – political decentralization. Leave it in.

Sentence 19: A detail about the political centralization mentioned in the paragraph above - the name of the city-state. Not a main point. Throw it out.

Now what have you left, after you've thrown out the unimportant paragraphs? Let's see.

Taking the title and section headings as they are, and further boiling down the first section headings as they are, and further boiling down the first sentence to a phrase or to each, this is what you should end up with:

THE GREEKS, I. BACKGROUND

Aegean Civilization Located at Crete, Troy and Mycenae. All made the same contributions. Contributions were in metals, building, engineering, art, politics, seafaring, warfare.

The Setting of Greek Civilization Greek civilization was shaped by (1) the forces of nature; (2) by

the easily navigable waters surrounding Greece; and (3) by the Greek terrain, which made for political decentralization.

With this online at your fingertips, you now begin reading the text to make sure understand each of these main points thoroughly.

However, had you not been able to get all the main points from the first six chapters signposts, you still had two more that might have been able to help you. Let's briefly glance at these now:

7. ILLUSTRATIONS

What they tell you: Illustrations, charts, graphs, photographs, etc., are pictorial presentations of the main ideas in each chapter. They boil down great amounts of information, and give them to you at a single glance. Often they convey information that simply could never be put into words.

For example: The map in sample chapter two shows at geographical setting of Greece quite vividly. At a glance, you see the wonderful advantages Greek mariners had to explore the entire Mediterranean. This confirms the main idea shown in the outline above concerning the easily navigable waters surrounding Greece.

And our last chapter signpost:

8. MARGINAL TITLES

What they tell you: Marginal titles take the main point of each paragraph, and set in bold type in the margin next to the text of the paragraph. They thus build a walking outline of the chapter for you in the margin. Unfortunately, however, they are not used in modern textbooks to any great extent; and you must get the same information from the paragraph heading mention above.

For example: None of our three sample chapters uses marginal titles. However, if our second sample chapter did use them, it would look like this:

3 "When copper and the manufacture of bronze were introduced, probably from Phoenicia or elsewhere in Asia Minor at some time before 3000 B.C, civilization began on Crete. The civilization is termed Minoan, from Minos,

legendary king, and archaeologists have divided it into three main chronological periods..."

IN SUMMARY:

When you are reading an individual chapter or lesson in a book, you use the same Pre-Reading, quick-survey technique that you first used to understand the book as a whole.

You use this quick-survey technique to pull out the main ideas from the chapter before you begin to read it.

You find these main ideas by checking the following eight chapter signposts:

1. The Chapter Title.
2. The Section Headings.
3. The Paragraph Headings or Bold Prints.
4. The Introductory Paragraphs.
5. The Summary Paragraphs.
6. The First Sentence Paragraphs.
7. The Illustrations.
8. The Marginal Titles.

When you lift these chapter signposts out of the text and arrange them in order, you will have an outline of the main thoughts of that chapter at your finger tips.

You may then flash-read that chapter – merely skimming over the unimportant details – and concentrating only on definite information on each of these main thoughts.

We now turn to a simply trick that will automatically show you exactly what information you must look for on each one of these main points.

CHAPTER 7

How to turn the chapter's main thoughts into questions, to automatically pinpoint the information you need about them

Now let's list the outlines you have built by Pre-Reading the three sample chapters in this book.

In the first sample chapter your outline will be as simple as this:

THE FOUR KIND OF SENTENCES

1. Declarative sentence.
2. Interrogative sentence.
3. Exclamatory Sentence.
4. Imperative Sentence.

In the second sample chapter, this is the outline you've worked out:

THE GREEKS, I. BACKGROUND

Aegean Civilization

Located at Crete, Troy and Mycenae. All made the same contributions.

Contributions were in metals, building, engineering, politics, seafaring, warfare.

The Setting of Greek Civilization.

Greek civilization was shaped by:

1. The forces of nature.
2. The easily navigable waters surrounding Greece.
3. The Greek terrain, which made for political decentralization.

And in the third sample chapter, the outline emerged like this:

FIVE ROADS TO COAST REDUCTION

1. Raw Materials.
2. Capital Equipment.
3. Manufacturing Costs.
4. Sales Expense.
5. General and Administrative Expense.

At this point, you have the main ideas of each sample chapter at your fingertips. But your knowledge of the chapter is, of course, still incomplete. Now you must read the text itself, to find what you should know about each one of these main points.

And how do you tell – again in advance of actually reading the text – exactly what it is that you should know about each one of these points?

The answer is simplicity itself. You merely

1. Turn each one of these main points into a question.

And then 2. Read the text to find out their answers. It's as easy as that. Now let's see this question-and-answer technique in action.

THE SIX BASIC QUESTIONS

Any idea – any word, any phrase, any sentence – can be turned into a question simply by putting in front of it one of these six little words:

What?
Why?
Where?
When?
Who?
How?

These are extremely valuable words. You should memorize them from this moment on. They have been called, and rightly so, the Six Tiny Keys to Knowledge. Let's see what they can do when we apply them to the main thoughts in each one of our sample chapters.

TURNING THE FIRST SAMPLE OUTLINE INTO A SERIES OF QUESTIONS

First, you start with the chapter title. Placing the word what in front of it, you get:

What are the four kinds of sentences?

This question has already been answered for you by the section headings in your online – declarative, interrogative, exclamatory, and imperative. So you put the same question to each of these four kinds of sentences, like this:

What is the definition of a declarative sentence? What is the definition of an interrogative sentence? What is the definition of an exclamatory sentence? What is the definition of an imperative sentence?

You now know exactly what information you are looking for about each one of your main points. You now read to answer these questions, to discover that information, and skim over everything else.

TURNING THE SECOND SAMPLE OUTLINE INTO A SERIES OF QUESTIONS

Again, you first start with the chapter title. Placing the word what in front of it, you get:

What are the background sources of Greek civilization?

This question has already been answered for you in the two section headings – the Aegean civilization and the geographical setting. So you question each one of the section headings in turn, like this:

Placing the word where in front of the first section heading, you get:

Where was Aegean civilization located?

Your paragraph headings answer this question – at Crete, Troy and Mycenae. So you ask again:

What were their contributions to Greek civilizations?

Again you have the answers – in metals, building, engineering, politics, seafaring, warfare. So you ask again:

What did the Aegean civilization contribute to the Greek Civilization in metals?

What did it contribute in building? What did it contribute in engineering? What did it contribute in politics? What did it contribute in seafaring? What did it contribute in warfare?

These are the questions in this section that you will read on to answer. You then turn to the second section, and question its heading.

What were the geographical factors that helped shape Greek civilization?

You have the answers – forces of nature, navigable waters, rough terrain. So you question each one of these factors in turn.

How did the forces of natures help shape Greek civilization? How did navigable waters help shape Greek civilization? How did the rough terrain help shape Greek civilization?

You know exactly what information you are looking for about each one of your main points. You now read to answer these questions, to discover that information, and skim over everything else.

TURNING THE THIRD SAMPLE CHAPTER INTO A SERIES OF QUESTIONS

Once again, you first start with the chapter title. Placing the word what in front of if, you get:

What are the five roads to cost reduction?

Your section headings give you the answers – raw materials, capital equipment, manufacturing costs, sales expense, and general and administrative expenses. So you question each one of these section headings in turn, like this:

How can my firm cut raw materials costs? How can my firm cut capital equipment costs? How can my firm cut manufacturing costs? How can my firm cut sales costs? How can my firm cut general and administrative costs?

You now know exactly what information you are looking for about each one of your main points. You now read to answer these questions, to discover this information, and skim over everything else.

IN SUMMARY:

In order to Pre-Read a chapter or an assignment, you follow three steps:

1. You check the chapter signposts.
2. You use them to pull out the main thoughts of the chapter.
3. You turn those main ideas into questions.

You do this by pleasing the words, what, why, where, when, how, or who in front of the thoughts. And when you have turned them into questions, and skim over everything else.

Let us now see how you slash through that text, mastering its content, without repetition, in a single flash reading.

CHAPTER 8
How to power-read – master an assignment in minutes

You have now finished your quick survey of the chapter. You have pulled out its main thoughts and turned them into questions. You are now ready to read text, word by word, to answer these questions.

Let's see how you do this, in the shortest possible time, without missing a single a vital point.

HOW TO DOULBE YOUR READING RATE

Always, of course, our first goal is to improve your ability to understand everything you read. But this search for understanding does not conflict with a second vital goal – to speed up your reading rate.

Fast readers are good readers. And most people who read slowly do so because of one or two crippling habits they've picked up in their School years. Eliminate those habits and you liberate tremendous new- reading speed in yourself overnight.

Since you will be faced with a flood of paperwork in your lifetime, now is the time to build in that speed. Here are five simple tricks that will do it for you automatically:

1. Don't let yourself point out words with your finger or a pencil. This slows you up. Read with your eyes only. This means your hands must be folded till you turn to the next page.

2. Keep from moving your lips or mouth. Lip-moving slows reading speed down to speaking speed. If it's difficult for you to stop moving your lips, bite a pencil while you read till you lose the habit.
3. Don't move your head from side to side. This tires you out and again slows up your reading. Only your eyes should move. Only your eyes need move.
4. Read aggressively. Actively. Tearing the ideas out of the pages with the techniques we are showing you in this book.
5. Learn the habit of skimming and then concentrating as described below. Make every reading assignment a search for main thoughts through a forest of useless words. Skim through 90 per cent those words, and concentrate only on the vital 10 per cent.

And then practice. Practice-practice-practice. Till you become an expert. Till these habits become second nature. Till you can zip through any written page, anywhere.

Like this:

HOW TO FLASH_READ. CUT THROUGH UNIMPORTANT DETAILS IN SECONDS

Now with these speed-reading skills firmly implanted in your mind as automatic habits, you begin to attack the chapter, word by word.

You begin to read as fast as you can. You read every word. But now you are sifting those words – judging them – accepting them or rejecting them.

You are looking for specific answers to specific questions – the questions you constructed in your quick survey before you began to read.

These questions are burned into your mind:

What is the forces of nature that helped shape Greek civilization? How can my firm cut raw materials costs?

Every word, every phrase, every sentence that your eye flashes over is judged by whether they answer or do not answer those questions.

If they answer the question, you stop, concentrate, underline as shown below.

If they do not answer the questions, you read on, searching for your answers.

In this way, you merely skim over 90 per cent of the text – the unimportant 90 per cent – the excess details, the side issues, the interesting opinions and prejudices that will never be needed again.

You read them quickly, once. You skip none of them. You let them register in your brain as they will. You let them fill in the details of the vital points you will later concentrate on. You make no deliberate conscious effort to memorize any of them.

But – because at the same time you are building up a structure of one vital thought in the chapter after another – you will find that these skimmed – over details, somehow automatically, stick to these main thoughts.

You will find that you remember far more of this chapter – main thoughts and details – than you have ever remembered before.

The reason for this increase in memory is simple. We remember what we can understand and what we can organize. If we try to memorize nonsense words or jumbled sentences, for example, we find it almost impossible. And a chapter that is not broken down into main thoughts and details is really nothing but a meaningless jumble.

But once you pick out its main thoughts and put them in order, you have constructed a memory framework. From that moment on you have a logical structure, a definite pigeonhole, for details to attach themselves to in your memory.

Then, even though you skim over these details and concentrate only on consciously memorizing your main thoughts, the details logically stick along to their parent thoughts, and you get them in your mind as a sort of no-work bonus.

So you have now flash-read 90 per cent of the chapter simply glanced at the details to pick them up –and are now ready to go to work on your main thoughts.

Here's how you do it

THE MAGIC KEY TO CONCENTRATION

As you remember, you are reading to find specific answers to specific questions. Every sentence you read is judged on that basis. Does it answer your questions, or does it not?

If it does not, you flash-read it, and search on for your answers.

If it does, however, you slow down, concentrate full attention on that sentence, and pick up your pencil to underline the answer.

This deliberate physical act – this aggressive underlining answers in the textbook as they are read – is the Golden Rule that makes your concentration automatic.

It converts routine reading into active, physical thought. It prevents your mind from wandering. It makes the dead, lifeless material in the book come to life with the thrill of personal discovery. It forces you to weed out, judge, emphasize. It is the first great step in turning that material into your own personnel acquisition as you hammer it out, answer by answer by answer.

And it is as easy as ABC. There is only one simple procedure to follow.

Every time you find the answer to one of your questions, you simply:

- Read it care fully
- Make sure you understand it. And
- Under line once the specific words you're going to use to remember it.

That's all there is to it. On an entire page you may underline only one or two sentences. In a complete lesson, you may make only four or five marks in your book.

But these physical marks are your own personal milestones along the road to mastery of that lesson. They are the first active steps, not only to locating the vital thoughts of that chapter, but to making those thoughts part of your mental inventory for as long as you wish to use them.

Let's see how this underlining process takes place. Let's put it to work on each of our three sample chapters.

HOW TO POWER-READ THE FIRST SAMPLE CHAPTER

Let's take the first paragraph of the first sample chapter. Here's how it now stands in the textbook:

"A declarative sentence makes a statement. It is followed by a period."

Here's how it should look when you have finished reading it:

"A declarative sentence makes a statement. It is followed by a period."

You have underlined four words and weeded out the rest. You now know the first kind of sentence and its definition. You have answered your first question. You now go on to the second, and the third, and the fourth, till you have finished the lesson.

HOW TO POWER-READ THE SECOND SAMPLE CHAPTER

In this chapter, let's take paragraph 17 as our example. Here's how it now stands in the textbook:

"The Greek homeland, however, had one great geographical advantage: its situation encouraged navigation, even by the rather timid. The irregular coasts of the mainland and the islands provided sheltered anchorages; destruction storms seldom occurred during the long summer, the great season of navigation; and the vessels could go for hundreds of miles without ever losing sight of land.

Travel in ships propelled by sails or oars or a combination of the two was cheaper, swifter and more comfortable than an uphill and down- dale journey overland. The Greeks, consequently, built up an active maritime trade."

As you remember, your Pre-Reading survey had already established the question you were searching for in this section. Here is that question:

How did navigable waters help shape Greek Civilization? With that question in mind, here is how this same paragraph should look when you have finished reading it:

"The Greek homeland, however, had one great geographical advantage: its situation encouraged navigation, even by the rather timid. The irregular coasts of the mainland and the islands provide sheltered anchorages; destructive storms seldom occurred during the long summer, the great season of navigation; and the vessels could go for hundreds of miles without ever losing sight of land.

Travel in ships propelled by sail or oars or a combination of the two was cheaper, swifter and more comfortable than up-hill and down- dale journey overland. The Greeks, consequently, built up an active maritime trade."

You have underlined eight words, and weeded out the rest. These eight words answer your question completely – allow you to realize that the navigable waters surrounding Greece enabled the Greeks to build up an active maritime trade. This is the main thought of this paragraph. The rest is merely detail.

And so you continue with your reading, using this same technique to weed out 95 per cent of the unimportant words in the chapter; to concentrate only on the answers to your main-thought questions; and to build up, answer by answer, the complete, easily remembered Main Thought Outline of this lesson, which we will examine in the next chapter.

HOW TO POWER-READ THIRD SAMPLE CHAPTER

As a contrast, let's take paragraph 24 of this chapter. Here's how it stands in the textbook:

"The fifth avenue of cost reduction consists of analysis of general and administrative expenses. In the normal company these cover such items as salaries of executives and office employees, office expense, interest, property depreciation, taxes, insurance, donations, legal fees, consultants, investigation of possible mergers, economic services and other general business expense."

Here the answer to the question gives eleven or more ways to cut costs in this area, and all are underlined. Later, when you build your Main Thought Outline, you will combine several of them so they can be more easily memorized.

At the present point, however, you continue to read on until you have finished the chapter, answered each of your questions and thoroughly understand each of its main points.

IN SUMMARY:

Once you have made your Pre-Reading survey, with its questions to be answered, the actual reading of the lesson becomes incredibly fast and easy.

During this reading, you will skim over about 90 per cent of the text, searching only for the answers to your main thought questions, and letting their details stick to your memory automatically.

And when you find a main-thought answer, you actively underline it, making each word that you will use later to remember it by.

In this way, you actively build up a series of main-thought answers, which you will now use to build a Main Thought Outline in your notebook so you can remember them as long as you wish.

It is to this last step of rewriting and remembering that we now turn.

CHAPTER 9
Note taking. How to remember what you've read and put it to immediate use

You are now ready for the pay-off, the moment when you master the meaning of the chapter and make it your own.

What have you done so far? All this:

1. Picked out the main thoughts of the chapter.
2. Turned them into questions.
3. Weeded out material that did not answer those questions, and which you will never have to look at again.
4. Located the answers to those questions – the vital information that composes the back bone of that book.
5. Marked that vital information separate from the rest of the chapter.

You now have everything you need to know about every main thought in that chapter, in your own personal language, making fifty words do the work of five thousand.

Now you rewrite the chapter, in your own personal language, making fifty words do the work of five thousand.

YOUR NOTEBOOK, WHERE YOU RE-CREATE THE BACKBONE MEANING OF EACH CHAPTER, EACH BOOK, EACH COURSE

In addition to you own mind, you have only three basic tools to open up the entire world of knowledge to your grasp:

Your textbook. Your pencil. And your notebook.

In fact, future advancement may very well depend on your ability to transfer knowledge from one of these books to the other.

What exactly is this notebook of yours? What should it contain? How should it be arranged? How exactly do you use it to get the maximum benefit from your reading?

Let's look at each of the points in turn.

Your notebook is the actual storehouse of all that you have learned, from every one of you books.

That notebook should be large and loose-leafed. It should have a durable hard cover. It should have plastic colour separators for each course. It should have your name, address, and telephone number written in ink inside the front cover, because it is much too valuable to lose.

When you sit down at your study table at home at night, it should be the first book you open. It is your portable organizer. It sets up your entire study schedule, in this way:

If you are going to an adult education class, for example, or taking a correspondence course, each course in the notebook must be set off by a plastic coloured separator. The first page following that separator is the assignment for each day is copied down exactly as it is given by your teacher, like this:

Chapter 2: "Five Roads to Cost Reduction. Answer questions 1 to 8 at end of chapter, to hand in tomorrow.

Each day's assignments are written in this way on the assignment page, one after another. As they are completed, they are checked off with a red pencil. But they are kept in the notebook, to serve as part of the flash review you will make before you take any test.

HOW YOU WRITE UP EACH DAY'S LESSON IN YOUR NOTEBOOK

After the assignment page, for each course, come the Main Thought Outline pages you will write up, day after day, as you master that course.

These pages are not haphazard in any way. They are not written in the classroom, not written while you are actually reading the text. There is no room on them for illegible scrawls, written daydreaming, or doodles of any kind.

They are carefully and precisely prepared, in this way:

1. When you have finished reading the chapter, and when you have underlined the answers to the main-thought questions that you have prepared, you then close the book.
2. You are now ready to put your knowledge of the backbone of that chapter to its first test. To do this, you take a blank sheet of paper – not in your notebook – and from memory you write down each of the main thoughts of that chapter and the information you have learned about them.

3. You will forget some of these points. You will write down some of them out of order. You will find that you still don't clearly understand some of the information about them. None of this is important. What is important is the fact that you have just made you first recitation, taken your first self-test on that chapter.
4. You now go back to the text and check and correct your outline. You write the corrections directly onto that rough outline.
5. When you have finished it, when you have boiled down and correctly arranged to your own satisfaction, then you turn that paper over. You open your notebook. And you write that outline – again from memory – on one page of that notebook.
6. What you are doing is freeing yourself, step by step, from the crutch of that textbook. You are transferring knowledge out of that textbook into your own memory, and then into your notebook for instant reference. And each step of the way you are condensing that knowledge, memorizing and rememorizing it, understanding it more deeply and clearly with each word you write.
7. When you have finished writing the outline in your notebook, you check it again. If there are one or two errors or omissions, write them in. If there are too many, rewrite the entire page. Write only one side of the paper, however, because you will use the other side later to double the profit you get out of every hour of review.

And then, when you have the outline in your notebook finished to your satisfaction, close both books and finish for the night. You have learned your chapter. You have the backbone of that chapter stored in your memory and your notebook, ready to go to work for you at an instant's notice.

Let's see what these finished outlines should look like, for each one of our sample chapters:

THE FINISHED OUTLINE FOR OUR FIRST SAMPLE CHAPTER

THE FOUR KINDS OF SENTENCE:

1. Declarative – makes a statement.
2. Interrogative – asks something.
3. Exclamatory – shows surprise or excitement.
4. Imperative – gives a command.

THE FINISHED OUTLINE FOR OUR SECOND SAMPLE CHAPTER The Greeks, I. The Background

1. Aegean Civilization. Centered at Crete, Troy, Mycenae.

Contributions were:

- Copper and bronze basis for high civilization.
- Advanced engineering techniques produced fortifications and palaces.
- Rules by kings
- Empire building through trade and warfare by sea.

2. Geographical Influences:

Poor soil and climate forced Greeks to seek their fortunes overseas. Easy navigability made sea transportation easier and more profitable than land. Rough terrain encouraged individual city-states.

THE FINISHED OUTLINE FOR OUR THIRD SAMPLE CHAPTER FIVE ROADS TO COST REDUCTION

1. Cut raw materials cost by:

- Precise purchasing specifications.
- Inspection of incoming materials.
- Elimination of manufacturing difficulties due to raw materials.
- Substitution or elimination of unnecessary materials.
- Financial control of sources.

2. Cut capital equipment costs by:

- Reducing costs of depreciation, replacement, maintenance and interest.
- Holding down inventories.
- Sharpening accounting procedures.

3. Cut manufacturing costs by:

- Better labour management.
- Analysis of indirect costs.
- Design of new equipment.
- Better working conditions.
- Improved materials handling.
- Operations research.

4. Cut sales costs by cutting costs of:

- Warehousing.
- Transportation.
- Advertising.
- Packaging.
- Direct sales costs.
- New specialist costs.

5. Cut general and administrative costs:

- Administrative salaries.
- Office expense.
- Interest.
- Insurance.
- Donations
- Legal fees.
- Consultants and other economic services.

TIPS ON IMPROVING YOUR OUTLINES

1. Simplify. Keep compressing, boiling down, making the outline shorter and shorter. Use phrases instead of sentences. Eliminate unnecessary words and details. Blend subordinate sentences into others by boiling them down into one or two words. Keep cutting till each idea stands sharp and clear in a few easy-to-remember words.
2. Fit the ideas together properly. Make sure one leads into the other in the right order. Then, when you think of the first idea, the second automatically pops into your mind.
3. What are the kinds of order you can use to make one idea fit in with another? Here are a few:

Example: Kinds of birds:

1. Sparrow
2. Robin
3. Bluebird, etc

Example: Battles of World War II :

1. Poland.
2. Holland.
3. France.
4. Britain, etc.

Example: How to Build a Work Bench:

A. Parts of Something.
B. Time Order.

1. Check each part and arrange in order.

C. Step-by-Step Sequence.

2. Read instructions carefully.
3. Cut out all parts, etc.

D. Causes of Something

Example Causes of 1929 Depression:

1. Watered stock
2. Insufficient government control.
3. Speculation by banks, etc.

E. Effects of Something

Example Results of 1929 Depression:

1. Vast unemployment.
2. Business bankruptcies.
3. Loss of 1932 election, etc.

Example: States on the Eastern Seaboard:

1. Maine.
2. Vermont
3. New Hampshire.
4. Rhode Island, etc.

F. Arrangement by Space

These are only a few samples. Look for other kinds, and keep a list of them at the back of your notebook.

4. Use numbers. They are a great help, both in understanding a lesson and remembering it for future use. For example, once you know that there are five roads to cost reduction, you realize that you must reproduce all five of them on any future test. If you had not numbered them, however, you may have thought there were only four, and left one out because you didn't stop to search for it.

5. Indent. And then indent again. Physical indentions show instantly the difference between the theme of the entire chapter and its sub-thoughts. And if these sub-ideas have any further divisions, again indentions show their relation at a glance.

Notes should be neat and precise, with plenty of white space around each point, so you can see exactly where it stands in relation to the chapter as a whole when you review it.

HOW TO USE YOUR NOTES

When you finish writing up these notes each night, you have accomplished not one but two vital tasks:

1. You have read and understood the chapter assigned to you – and understood it more completely than you have ever dreamed before.
2. You have stored away the backbone meaning of that chapter – so that you can now thoroughly review it for a test by reading as few as fifty words, instead of as many as five thousand.

You have two enormous advantages over every other person in your class who does not use this technique. And you begin putting those advantages to use immediately.

Your first review takes place right after you finish those notes, in your ten-minute review that same evening. Here you discover exactly how much you have gained from your day's reading. Here you put this new knowledge to work before you enter your class the next evening.

The procedure is simple. You put away your notes from memory, then try to rewrite them from memory.

You should be able to write all those notes from memory, without referring back to your original copy.

If not, reread the original notes until each point in them is clear in your mind. Then test your over-all mastery of the course by asking yourself these questions, which force you to tie in your daily reading with everything you have learned before:

"Why did the author place this chapter where it is in the book?"

"How does it tie in with the chapter I read yesterday?"

"What did I have to know in yesterday's chapter before I could understand the material I read today?"

These questions force you to think. To tie in. To relate forward and backward. And to become accustomed to expressing your thoughts in your own words.

When you are through with that simple review each night, you know that you have mastered that material. And you're confident that you can talk sense about it to anyone.

THE NEXT EVENING

And the next evening, on your way to class, take one brief look over these notes. Driving to school, walking through the halls, with your notebook closed, run through these three magic questions:

"In one sentence, what did I learn from last night's chapter?" (That the five roads to cost reduction are through reducing raw materials costs, manufacturing costs, capital equipment costs, sales costs, and general and administration costs.)

"IIow does this tie in which the chapter before?" (It's a second way of increasing profits, right after improved management.)

"What questions will I be asked on it in next week's test?" (To list several ways of reducing costs in each one of these areas. And run through them.)

Using this planning technique, in half the time that it would have taken you to read that chapter before, you are now ready to go in that classroom and make your friend eyes pop open in amazement.

IN SUMMARY:

There is an easy, simple, organized way to master the contents of any assignment. It consists of the following three steps:

1. Pre-Read the assignment, to pick out its main thoughts and turn them into questions.
2. Power-read the assignment, to weed out unnecessary details and concentrate on the answers to these questions.
3. Translate the assignment into a Main Thought Outline that expresses these answers in as few words as possible, and that is stored for instant review in your notebook.

These are the three Magic Keys to Expert Reading. You should practice them again and again and again, until they become second nature. They will pay you dividends for the rest of your life.

CHAPTER 10
How to get twice as much out of your daily reading

Now let's put these reading skills to work for you in another area.

Let's see how they can save you time and effort every single day. Double the amount of information you get out of a magazine or newspaper. Cut your business reading time in half. Let you flash right through the latest best-seller- and dazzle your friends that same evening with the insights you have into every one of its events and characters.

Let's start with the Number One source of information for most people – your newspaper:

HOW THE PROFESSIONALS READ THEIR NEWSPAPER

You need two separate skills – two separate patterns of action – to get the most out of your daily paper:

1. How to read your newspaper as a whole.
2. How to read each individual news story that catchers your eye.

First, let's set up an over-all pattern of attack – a timed, step-by- step procedure – that will tear out all the important facts from your paper for you every evening or morning.

Here's how we do it – step by step:

1. When you open your newspaper in the morning, the first thing you do is skim all the headlines on the front page. (Or, if you read a tabloid, skim all the headlines of the first four or five pages.)

What you are trying to achieve here – with this first rapid, over-all view of the headlines – is "to see the world in one piece." To get a bird's- eye view of all the important events of the day at one time. And to see – if possible – how each of these events ties in to all the others.

For example, consider the fateful week of October 12, 1964. Scanning the typical newspaper of any day that week, you would see that the Labour government had just been elected in England... that Khrushchev had been pushed out of the Soviet government... that Red China had exploded an atomic bomb... that Johnson and Goldwater were battling for the presidency of the United States.

Now, what does this bird's-eye view show you? First of all – change! Country after country is changing internally. And the balance of power itself is changing externally. But exactly how? How rapidly? Towards What?

How do these events tie in to each other? What is the connection between Khrushchev's fall from power and the Chinese bomb? What effect will both these events have on the American election?

This first two-minute glance tells you what happened on that day, and leads you to set up questions in your mind about why it happened, and what effect one event will, have on the other.

You now read to answer these questions. You do it in this way:

HOW TO READ A NEWS STORY

2. Now you start on the articles themselves. Your objective here is to get the big facts – the important facts- out of each story as fast as you can, without missing a single vital detail.

You do this by going back to the headline, and turning it into a series of questions. For example:

KHRUSHCHEV REMOVED FROM POWER

Bring these questions to mind: Why?

How?
By Whom?

What was done with him? What will happen next? Or this headline:

RED CHINA EXPLODES A-BOMB

Bring these questions to mind: How big was it?

How powerful?

How many does china have?

Was it a real bomb, or just a test device?

Does China have the means to drop it overseas? What will happen next?

Now – with these questions in mind – read the first paragraph of the story. This first paragraph is actually complete summary of the story. It gives you an outline of what follows. It should answer most of your questions – along with Who?... What?... When?... Where?... Why?... and How?

Now, in most stories, this first (or second, or third) paragraph should give you as much information as you want to know. In other words, it should answer your questions – at least in outline form.

However, if you wish to gain more information on any one of these points, read on. Each of the paragraphs that follow should be an expansion of one of the main points summarized in the first paragraph. You skim each paragraph till you find that point mentioned again, and then read it carefully to pick up the details you want.

This way, there is no waste reading, and no waste time. You simply:

1. Read the headline.
2. Frame the questions you want answered about the details in that story.
3. Read the first one or two paragraphs to answer those questions.
4. And then read on only to pick up details on those points with vitally interest to you.

By using this system you can get the guts of a story in a minute or two. And then you're ready to go on and

LEARN THE BACKGROUND BEHIND THE NEWS

3. Now – when you've read the important news of the day, and its important details – you now turn to the sections of your paper that tell you:

What does it all mean?

Now you get the comment of skilled interpreters to unravel this news and help you with your own opinions. So you next read the columnists whose job it is to assign meanings to these events.

And then you turn to the editorial pages where the paper itself interprets the news and takes stands on the major issues of the day. And where readers like yourself air their reactions in their letters to the editors.

Now – how do you pull out the gist of these many interpretations in only a few minutes each day? By reading them like this:

An editorial is built up differently from a news story. In a news story the conclusion comes first; the details later. In an editorial, however, the writer begins by reciting facts you already know – by reviewing the situation to make it fresh in your mind. And then he goes on to state his own conclusion. Or solution. Or what he wants you to think and so you read a column or editorial backwards. You read the last paragraph first, to see if you can't pick up his interpretation.

Then you jump to the front. Skim rapidly through the first paragraphs. Look only for background facts that you don't know... reasons to support his interpretation... what he thinks will happen next.

Only a few minutes for each column, and you're through with the main news of the day. But look what you've accomplished! You've not only got the facts down solid, but you've formed your own opinions, and you've got plenty of good, solid, clearly-thought-through ideas to back them up!

With this technique, you'll never be at sea in a serious discussion again. You'll know exactly where you stand on important issues. You'll think straight on crucial decisions – be able to vote more intelligently – lead other's opinions on issue after issue.

AND NOW GO ON TO FINISH THE PAPER

4. Now turn to the index. Review the minor stories. Pick out the subjects of special interest to you – sports, business, fashion, home, what have you.

Use the same headline-question-answer techniques on each story you glance at. Pull out the facts you want- in minutes.

If you read movie or stage or book reviews, use the same last-paragraph-first technique that you use on the editorials. Get the conclusion first. Then fill in whatever details interest you.

5. And when you're through with the paper, just don't throw it away and forget it. Think of the news as a continued story. Follow each story as it develops day by day. Always-try to anticipate what will happen next.

6. If you can, read at least two different papers a day. Try to get different viewpoints in each. Compare them. Find out where they differ. Sharpen your reasoning power. Judge for yourself which one is right.

7. And, of course, supplement your papers with radio, TV, lectures, books, etc.

Let's see how you put one of these "bonus media" to work – in half the time you're using today.

HOW TO FLASH-READ MAGAZINES

With magazines, your plan of attack is different. Here's how to read them most efficiently:

1. Start with the Table of Contents. Check off the articles that interest you most. Turn their titles into questions, and then turn to them.
2. Read each article's title and subtitle... the first paragraph... all subheads... and the last paragraph or two. This should give you the main idea, and enough information to tell you whether you want to read further or not.
3. If you do go further, again ask questions before you read word by word. Remember – magazines present more than mere fact; they also give you opinion. So, if you come across this kind of headline:

A PLAN TO FREE CUBA

Ask yourself these questions: What is it? Who is its author? How qualified is he?

What steps does his plan require? How long would it take? What are its chance of success? What would happen if it succeeded?

4. Also, remember that most magazine articles are trying to get you to feel, believe, or do something. Therefore, ask yourself:

> What reaction does this author want from me? How does he try to convince me that I should do this? What facts or arguments does he use to do this? What facts does he distort? What facts does he leave out? Where can I get the other side of this proposal?

5. To help you answer that last question, try to read at least two magazines – with as contrasting viewpoints as possible. Compare their interpretations. See what facts one leaves out that the other stressed. Form your own judgments.
6. Now skim through the article. Skip details. Get the main thoughts. Go on till you've answered your questions. And then turn to then next article.
7. When you've finished your main articles of interest, then quickly skim through the magazine, page by page. You may pick up something of interest that wasn't fully disclosed in the Table of Contents.
8. To read fiction in magazines, as in books, follow these rules:

HOW TO READ FICTION TWICE AS FAST, AND REMEMBER TWICE AS MUCH

1. Remember – all fiction is about people. Therefore, your first job is to get acquainted with the people in your book. Ask yourself: Who is the hero? Write his name on the front cover of the book. Describe him – his appearance and his character.

Who is the heroine? Write her name. Describe her. Jot down the character traits and desires that are going to determine her actions throughout the book.

Who is the villain? Describe him. List his motives. Tell why they're going to bring him in conflict with the hero.

Where are they all? Make sure you know the time and location of their surroundings.

What are they trying to do? What blocks them from doing it? What's going to happen next?

2. Read the first chapters carefully. They set the stage – forecast the ultimate outcome. Then read faster and faster as the characters become more familiar – as the action becomes more predictable.
3. Try to outguess the author. He's planted hints on what's going to happen at the end. Can you predict that end before he tells it to you? If you can, you'll not only get a tremendous kick out of it, but you'll learn how to see into people – predict what they'll do under stress. And this is the great benefit you're looking for from great fiction.
4. When you reach the end, ask: What happened? To whom? How did they change – for better or for worse?

What is the author trying to say? What moral is he pointing out? What kind of world does he say it is?

Is it true to life? Do you believe in his characters – in his events in his outcome? This is the ultimate test. When you've answered this question, you've told yourself whether you've just read great fiction, or pulp fiction.

And finally, what have you learned? What has this man, in this book, taught you about the way human beings act, feel, believe, fight, love, build and even die!

Never fool yourself. You can learn easily as much from fiction as you can from fact. And you can put these new insights... these new emotions... these new competencies in handling people – to work for you, the very same day!

5. Now read the reviews. Compare their judgments with yours. Search for the reasons these reviewers give for their judgments. Then see if your reasons hold up as well. If not, revise and strengthen them.
6. And now turn to the back cover of the book. Sum it up in one paragraph. Who did what - against what obstacles - and

with results? Try to boil down the entire experience – the entire moral – into one brief summary that will unlock the entire book for you again if you come back to it even a year later.

AND NOW TO CUT YOUR BUSINESS READING IN HALF

Business reading falls into two mains divisions – each of which has its own problems and its own techniques. These are:

1. Keeping up with your field.
2. Ploughing through a desk full of correspondence, memos, reports and what have you every day.

Let's take correspondence and the rest first. Here's how to lick it:

1. When you pick up a business letter, first glance at the letterhead – then immediately at the signature. (If it's a memo, look at the origin and content information at the top.)

Ask yourself these questions:

Who sent it to you?☐Do you know him? Do you know his company? What do you think he wants?☐What did you say in your last letter to him? What did you want him reply?

2. Now sweep down the letter with a glance. Most letters are usually very simple. They deal with one, two or three things. Can you see at a glance what they are? What the writer wants you to do?
3. Now read the last paragraph first. The information you want – what the writer wants you to do – should be summarized in the last paragraph.

4. Glance only briefly at the first paragraphs. They're usually filled with mere formalities ("We have your letter of the ... Thank you for... We note with great pleasure... etc.") Skip them. Get to the heart of the matter fast.

5. Concentrate your attention at mid-page. Here are the reasons why... the specific step-by-step that he wants done... the statements on which you'll have to base your decision with regard to this letter.

6. Now you can tell these facts about the letter:

Is it important? If not, glance briefly through the rest, and get rid of it.

Is it your department? If not, send it to the person whose job it is.

Does it demand an answer? If so, answer it there and then, so you won't have to read it twice.

Does it demand action? If so, delegate it immediately. Get it started at once.

7. In reading memos and reports, read them backwards. Look first at the point of origin and the man who wrote it. Then look immediately at the last page. See if it's summarized. This tells you whether it's worth your time, belongs to your department, has to be read thoroughly – or whether you can simply pick up the core of it from the summary and then pass it along to someone else.

READING BUSINESS ARTICLES AND TECHNICAL REPORTS

Business articles and technical reports have three main purposes:

To report on work in progress.

To detail particulars of some specific operation or method.

To describe new and modern approaches to the problems of the profession or field. Therefore, to keep up with your field with the least possible expenditure of time, you read them this way:

1. With a business journal, you follow the same first step as you did when reading any other kind of magazine. Read Table of Contents first. Mark the articles of interest. Read their summaries. Then decide if you'll read them thoroughly.
2. In reading a technical report, always define your purpose first. Tell yourself exactly why you're reading it. Exactly what you're looking for. Then disregard everything else.
3. Don't be fooled by their formidable appearance. Their organization is usually quite simple. Read the title. Then look for a summary – usually in the first paragraphs or the last.
4. Disregard footnotes. In nine cases out of ten, they're only for specialists.
5. Concentrate on getting the main ideas. Number them. If the report describes a new procedure, look for each important step. Number them.
6. You should be able to boil down each report, each article, into a main-idea summary no longer than an index card. (If you want to keep details, then save the article. File it with reference to the index card.)

    After you've boiled it down, turn the index card over and try to repeat its contents to yourself from memory. Try to get every numbered point in the proper sequence. This gives you a stronger grip on the article's organization and burns its main points into memory.
7. Now decide what to do with that information. Put it to work. Use it. Adapt it. Pass it on to others so they can understand you better when you call on them to back you up. Don't just file and forget it. New information means new ability-new power-new competence. In the long run-if it's put to use-it means new prestige and new money!

IN SUMMARY:

You can double the amount of reading you get done every day-
and remember twice as much of it - if you follow these simple
rules:

1. Look before you leap. Get the main idea first. Don't start
   reading word-by-word till you know it.
2. Ask questions. Read to answer them. Stop reading when
   you've got their answers.
3. Skip details. They'll only confuse you while you're reading
   - slip out of your mind as soon as you close the page.
   Concentrate on the core. Number it. Memorize it.
4. Then put it to work. Remember - new knowledge means
   new opportunity.

CHAPTER 11
The all-important art of listening-right down to reading the speaker's thoughts In addition to reading, you gain the information you need by listening.

In fact, in the business and social worlds, your ability to listen well is even important than your ability to read well. Most people gain about 80 per cent of all new facts through their ears, not their eyes.

Therefore hearing everything that is said, and missing nothing, is an indispensable art. But it is an art. It is not a natural gift. You must teach it to yourself. Just as you must learn how to read, so you must learn how to listen in this simple but tremendously powerful way:

HOW TO DEVELOP YOUR LISTENING POWER IN A FEW MINUTES EVERY NIGHT

When do you start to develop this ability to listen with the power of a tape recorder?

Start this way. Some night at the dinner table make up a new game for the family. Ask someone to read you a list of objects, cars, baseball players, the names of his friends what have you. Then try to name back that list in the order in which they gave it to you.

It's as simple as that. Start with a list of ten objects. Compete with your family. Award prizes. See how many you can name, and how much you can improve. At first you'll remember six or seven. Then eight or nine. Then all ten – perfectly.

As you go along, make the game harder. Have someone tell you a story, and repeat the important facts. Then a newspaper article. Ask them to try to stick you with specific names and figures. Watch yourself repeat them back, number by number.

You'll be astounded at how much you can retain. And how you've learned the first secret of good listening – strengthening your ear – channels memory – learning to remember everything important that you hear.

Now you're ready for the second step.

HOW TO CONCENTRATE ON THE SPEAKER'S THOUGHTS, AND NEVER BE DISTRACTED

Once you have strengthened your listening memory, so that you can hold entire thoughts and sentences in your mind after hearing them only once, you're ready to fit them together into meaningful patterns as the speaker talks.

There is a definite technique to re-creating the core of a lecture or conversation – any lecture or conversation – so that you need never forget it. Here's how:

Learning to listen well – to hear everything of real importance that's being said – is primarily a matter of being able to maintain attention. Of pacing yourself to follow the speaker's thoughts, and not letting your mind wander off. Because of this fact, the power of complete attention has been called the mark of an educated man.

Why is it difficult to maintain this attention? Because the human brain thinks about four times as fast as the human tongue can speak. And the huge gap between the speed of your mind and the words you are hearing provides time for all sorts of distracting personal thoughts.

How do you keep these distracting thoughts from leading you astray? By forcing yourself to keep pace with the speaker in these ways, every time you find your mind about wander:

1. By summarizing what the speaker has already said, and building it into a main-thought outline. Here you ask yourself questions like these:
   How can I sum up these statements in a single phrase? How do they tie in with his last point?
2. By anticipating the speaker's next point, with questions like these:
   What is he getting at here? Where will he go now? What examples must he give to prove this point?
3. By listening "between the lines" for points that are not put into words, with questions like these:

What is he implying there? Why does he stick to this one point, and not go on to the other we were discussing last week? Is he hinting at more than he's willing to say right out?

And so on, with other questions that will come to your mind as you seek the inner meaning of the speaker's words.

All these questions have one vital trait common. They turn listening from a passive to an active occupation. They stop drifting. They force you to think step by step with the speaker. To keep your mind constantly focused on that speaker's thoughts, both expressed and unexpressed. To literally pull the core meaning out of that lecture as it develops in front of you.

And then, as you do in your reading, night after night, you store that core meaning on paper so you can have it for good. In this way:

HOW TO TAKE LECTURE NOTES

You now have two powerful tools that enable you to capture the inner meaning of any spoken statement, lecture or conversation you may hear.

You have developed a strong listening memory, so you can hold entire thoughts and sentences in your mind after hearing them only once.

And you have the ability to keep your attention focused on the speaker's thoughts, both expressed and unexpressed, for as long as necessary to pull out the inner meaning of those thoughts as it develops in front of you.

In your formal education, you now make these two gifts even more effective by learning how to re-create the backbone meaning of any lecture you may attend – in your own notebook, where you will have it for instant reference whenever you need it.

Because a word is spoken once and then is lost forever, lecture notes are prepared differently from reading notes. Though the end result is the same, the technique of capturing the main thoughts must work far faster in the lecture hall, for example, than in the reading room.

Here is that technique, step by step:

1. The more you know about the material covered by a lecture, the more you will get out of the lecture. Therefore always read the material in the textbook before it's covered in the lecture. Then you can use at least part of the lecture as a review, rather than a new learning experience.
2. What you are looking for in such a lecture is enrichment. This is the material that the teacher includes in his lecture that is not in the textbook, and that can never be picked up by mere textbook reading alone. This bonus information should form the core of the lecture, and should be what you bring home in your notebook.
3. The lecture pages in your notebook should be separate from your reading pages. To begin with, of course, you will take your lecture notes on a piece of scrap paper, where you can jot down ideas as they seem important to you, and cross them out or rearrange them as you see corrections are necessary. Only after the lecture is over will you write them up in finished form and put them into your notebook, as we explain below.
4. These lecture notes begin the moment you walk into the room. You have already reviewed the textbook material you believe will be covered in the lecture; you are prepared to listen. Take a seat as far forward in the room as possible. Place your book and notebook on the floor, leaving on the desk only a piece of scrap paper and pen or pencil with which to write.
5. Write at the top of that paper the date, the name of the lecturer (if it is different from your regular teacher). And the subject of the lecture as soon as it is announced.
6. Your first goal is to discover the central theme, the main point, the speaker's goal in giving the lecture. You find this out in one of several ways:

It may be contained in the lecture title. A lecture on The Five Roads to Cost Reduction, for example, would give you the theme immediately.

If the title is vague, however, then you must look elsewhere. Perhaps the lecturer distributes notes on mimeographed sheets before the lecture. These should be carefully read and the main thoughts underlined. If the central theme is given on the sheet, it should be transferred to your note paper immediately.

If there are no printed notes, then you must listen carefully to the lecturer's opening remarks. You should, of course, disregard introductory acknowledgements, anecdotes, jokes, and so on, and concentrate on picking up such signal phrases as the following:

"I wish to discuss tonight the problem of - " "The theme of my lecture tonight will be - " "Have you ever thought of the extreme importance of this country of - "

Somewhere in these opening remarks, the main theme will emerge. As soon as you have it, it should be boiled down in your mind to one or two phrases, and written at the top of your paper. There it will control the development of your outline – tell you exactly what to look for in the rest of the lecture.

7. Once you know the main them of the lecture, your next goal is obvious. You must chart the development of that central theme through one vital thought after another. You are now building your outline from the speaker's words – listening for main thoughts and writing each of them down in order.

8. To do this you listen 90 per cent of the time and write the other ten. Note taking is not stenography. It is never merely writing down the exact words the lecturer uses, even if that were possible. Note taking is condensation. Judgment. Weeding out the unimportant. Boiling down the central thoughts, as they occur, to a few capsule words or phrases, and then fitting them into their place in your growing outline.

9. How do you recognize these main thoughts? In two ways. First because they are big ideas pertaining to the central theme of the lecture. (For example, in a lecture on The Five Roads to Cost reduction, once you have heard the speaker say, "Now, the first road to cost reduction is, of course, to cut raw materials cost," you would know that you had your first main thoughts.

10. Next, you recognize the lecture's main thoughts by the signal words are much like the chapter signposts that guide you to the meaning of your textbook reading. They are verbal signals that flag your attention, that warn you that something really important will follow them. Let's look at a few of them right now.

Any number is a direct giveaway that the speaker is going to list his main points for the audience. He may even give the audience advance notice of how many main points he's going to have, in this way:

"Now, the geographical setting of ancient Greece had three main influences upon Greek civilization."

At that point you mark in your rough notes:

Influences of geographical setting:

1...
....
2...
....
3...
....
....

You now know that there are three geographical influences, and you have set aside space for each of the three as they come up in the lecture. You now have a built-in main-thought trap in your notes. Listen without writing until the speaker signals again, by saying: "The first geographical influence –"

11. In addition to these automatic signal words that point out the main thoughts of the lecture, the speaker many times will pause, then tell the class that such and such a point is going to be asked for in a future test. He may use any one of the following forms to announce this:

"It is important to note – " "Be sure to know – " "Pay special attention to – " "Or he may come right out and say it: "You'll be asked to – "

This will be a test question – "

Once you hear these clues, set this point off from the rest of the lecture in this way. Mark a large TQ (for Test Question) beside it. Then, in your review later on, you can give it special attention.

HOW TO FINISH THE NOTES SO THEY CONTAIN EVERYTHING YOU NEED FROM THE LECTURE

12. Now what have you done so far during this lecture? You have: Written down the central theme at the top of your paper. Jot down the main headings as they were either outlined at the beginning of the lecture, or as they emerged during its development,

    Left plenty of room after each of these headings to serve as main-thought traps to pick up their vital sub-points,

    Filtered out these sub-points by careful, active listening and by following the clues the speaker's signal words gave you.

13. Therefore, at the end of the lecture, you should have the main-thought backbone of that lecture completely down on your rough sheet of paper. Now your job is to rewrite those notes into finished form as soon as possible.

14. If you have the time, stay in the lecture hall after the others have left, and rewrite them there. Use the first available five minutes to fix those notes firmly in your notebook and in your mind.

15. Rewrite them in this way. Reread everything you put down on the rough sheet of paper, making sure you understand each point and its relation to every other point in the lecture. Then, if necessary, put them in the correct and final order. Weed out. Number. Underscore. Organize. Until you have these notes written as clearly and completely as your reading notes every night.

16. This is your first self – recitation of the material in this lecture. When you have finished it, and when you have fitted it into place behind your other lecture notes, you have made that lecture your own. You are now ready to relate it to your reading notes on the same material, and put it to use whenever you need it for a test.

TWO OTHER VITAL CLASSROOM TECHNIQUES

At one time or another during a lecture, no matter how bright you are, you will have a moment when you just don't understand one of the speaker's statements, or when you have a thought that would modify that statement.

Therefore you must get into the habit of asking questions, of speaking up in the classroom.

If the teacher allows questions during the lecture, ask a brief, polite, to-the-point question immediately. This question should have one purpose: to clear up the point that is vague in your mind. Once it is cleared up, write the point and its answer in your rough notes, and check it later to make sure you have understood it. As we shall discuss later, any misunderstanding is a golden opportunity for learning.

If the teacher does not permit questions during the lecture, then speak to him after class. In any case, never leave the classroom with the question unanswered.

At the same time, if sample problems are done by the teacher during the lecture, copy them, word by word, right into your notebook.

This is essential – especially in your mathematics classes - for these two reasons:

First, because it trains you away from attempting your own short- cut methods, where you may leave out vital steps and get hopelessly lost. And it eliminates the necessity for you to copy answers rather than mastering the methods that produce them.

When you start to apply problem-solving techniques, there will be no pat answers to copy. Then only methods will be of any use. (And, if you are going to compete, you had darned well better know them.)

And secondly, this step-by-step copying of sample problems is one more way of assuring attentiveness. Again, the best way by far to learn, with a pencil in your hand.

IN SUMMARY:

Power-listening can be developed as effectively as Power-reading, simply by learning a few easy techniques. These are:

Strengthening you listening memory, so you can retain whole phrases, thoughts, and sentences in your mind after hearing them only once.

Teaching yourself to maintain full concentrated attention on the speaker's words, so that no important thought, expressed or unexpressed, can escape you.

And learning how to boil a lecture down into its vital thoughts, each in its proper order, so you can store the backbone meaning of the lecture in your mind and your notebook for instant reference whenever you need it.

PART THREE
Expressing the facts – writing and conversing

CHAPTER 12
The first essential – correct spelling made easy

In your day-to-day life, when you are submitting a resume for an important job, or writing an application for membership in a club, a single mistake in spelling can ruin the entire impression you are trying to make.

You cannot afford to be satisfied with anything less in your spelling than 100 per cent perfect. And it can be, if you follow these simple rules:

THE WRONG AND RIGHT WAYS TO IMPROVE YOUR SPELLING

In the first place, don't try to improve your spelling by going over lists of misspelled words and trying to correct them. These lists only concentrate your attention on the wrong spelling.

Instead, focus your efforts on the right spelling, in the right way, like this:

Realize that the reason you misspell any word is because you have a distorted image, and replace it with the correct one in such a way that it is burned forever into your memory.

You do this in three simple steps:

First, you see that word in such a way that the correct spelling of the hard part of the word sticks out like a sore thumb.

Second, you learn simple spell-alikes for the hard part of the word that brings the right spelling of it automatically to your mind every time.

And third, you write that word twice as large as you ordinarily write, until you get the correct feel of the word forever implanted in them muscles of your arm.

Not only are these three correction steps simple and easy, they are also enormous fun. Let's see how each of them works:

STEP ONE: SEE THE HARD PART OF THE WORD CORRECTLY

As you know, most words that are misspelled are misspelled in only one place in the entire word. Either you have added a letter where it shouldn't be, or forgotten one where it should be, or put in an e for a, or doubled a letter when it should remain single, or some other simple mistake.

But, once you have developed that distorted image of the word, then it sticks in your mind. You misspell that word over and over again, always in the same way, always in the same place.

From that moment on, there is a part of that word that you automatically misspell. It is that hard part on which you now concentrate.

First, you check over your writing and pick out the misspelled words. Then you locate the hard part of each of those words – the one or two letters in it that you automatically misspell.

And then you rewrite that word correctly – this time CAPITALIZING those hard letters.

You write it like this:

climb
borrow
Unable
parallel
tomoRRow arGUMent, and so on.

Now, copy this correct spelling on a second sheet of paper – over and over again – with the capitals in exactly the same place that you have put them.

Write that word over and over and over again – capitals and all – until you've got it down pat. Until you can see the correct capitalized spelling of the hard part of that word with your eyes shut.

Then you've completed your first step. You're well on your way to perfect spelling.

STEP TWO: BUILD AN AUTOMATIC MEMORY PROMPTER TO SPELL THE HARD PART OF THE WORD CORRECTLY

Now, you are going to reinforce that correct picture image of that word in your mind. You are going to do it by creating a simple spell-alike to help you remember how the difficult letters go.

You are going to create an automatic memory tie-in between the difficult part of the word and an easy-to-remember spell-alike, like this:

There are three different ways to create these spell alikes. Try them in the following order, until you get one that you automatically remember.

First of all, look for familiar words within the hard words, to make them easy to remember. Make up little sentences that tie these familiar words and the hard words together. For example:

"The SECRET was kept by the SECRETary." "After I ATE, I was grateful." "We will GAIN a bargain." "It's VILE to allow special privilege." "Scientists LABOR in a LABORatory."

120

Second, if there are no familiar words within the hard words, then look for the same part in smaller familiar words.

For example:

"We write a lettER on our stationERy." "When we PARt, we separate." "Please BRing the umBRella."

Finally, if neither of these first two rules works, then make up pure spell-alikes- as funny and as nonsensical as possible. For example:

"She screamed EEE as she passed the cEmEtEry." "The RR train and I had a quaRRel."

"GM uses good judgment."

"I gave HER HER handkerchief."

"I say BR when I think of FeBRuary."

There is a spell-alike for every misspelled word. One of these three rules will turn up the right one for you. Remember, keep them as vivid and as funny as possible; in that way, they'll be much easier to remember.

And, once you're on to the game, let the whole family think up the spell-alikes. It's not only great fun to see who can come up with the most outlandish ones, but it's marvellous training for future creativity.

And, always, it makes the correct spelling of those difficult words automatic, as soon as the spell-alike flashes into your mind to tell you the way those hard letters should go.

STEP THREE GET THE ARM-FEEL OF WRITING THAT HARD WORD CORRECTLY

Now after you've capitalized the hard part of that misspelled word, and after you've thought up a spell-alike to remember its correct order automatically, then you are ready to build the correct spelling of the word into a written reflex without even think of it.

Here's how:

Take a piece of blank, unruled paper. Write the word in natural script, without the capital letters, across thc top of the paper. But this time write it TWICE AS BIG as you ordinarily would.

TWICE AS BIG, over and over and over again. Write it without looking at it. Never hesitate. Never stop in the middle. If you get the word wrong, run through the first two steps again. And then go back to the TWICE AS BIG written immediately.

Over and over again. Until you build the writing of that word into a mechanically perfect skill. Until you get the word down letter-perfect. Until you build the writing of that word into a mechanically perfect skill. Until you can write it correctly as casually as you write your own signature.

Then it belongs to you. You have it – forever.

HOW TO MAKE THIS THREE-STEP SYSTEM WORK FOR YOU EVERY DAY!

To learn a new word, as we have said before, means to know its meaning, its use in a sentence, its correct pronunciation, and its correct spelling. Until all these are letter perfect, you really don't own the word at all.

As you advance through your business and social life, you will meet more and more important new words. Some of them you will misspell. Therefore you should have a Spelling Section in the back of your notebook. I suggest that you keep this Spelling Section for your reading notes and/or home-study courses.

Divide this section into two parts. Title the first part "Misspelled Words," and mark down in it any word you misspell.

Every night take one of these misspelled words – no more – and use the system to teach yourself its correct spelling.

Then when you have had that word letter-perfect, list it in the second part of the Spelling Section under the title "Mastered Words."

When you have listed about ten or twelve of these mastered words, have someone dictate all of them to you in a short paragraph or story. Then check each of their spellings.

If any are misspelled, put them back in the first part of the Section, and start all over again, because you haven't established the correct habit yet.

But you will. Before you know it, you'll be amazed at the absolute precision you show in these spelling tests.

And once you have mastered a word, use it as often as possible. This will help you practice, to keep the confidence – show you over and over again that you no longer have the slightest reason to be afraid of misspelling that once terrifying word.

IN SUMMARY:

There's only one permissible way to spell; that is 100 per cent, letter-perfect.

This can be easily done if you correct every spelling error, individually, with this simple three-step method:

1. Detect the one or two letters in each difficult word that you automatically spell wrong. Then CAPITALIZE the correct spelling of those letters till they stick out in front of your eyes like a sore thumb.
2. Think up spell-alikes for the hard letters that automatically remind you of the correct way those hard letters should go.
3. And then get the feel of hand spelling the word right, over and over and over again, twice as big as life, till you jot it down correctly as easily and as automatically as you write your name.

This three-step system, applied daily to master one misspelled word, will make you a spelling whiz in far less time than you believed possible.

And now we turn to your ability to express thoughts on paper – professional writing secrets that will enable you to turn in top-grade letters, memos, speeches, sales presentations, reports and what-have-you almost as fast as the words can form in your mind.

CHAPTER 13
How to write as easily and quickly as you think

The farther you advance in the business and social world, the more you will be required to prepare resumes, interoffice memos, engineering reports, business and social letters, club minutes, and much, much more.

All of this vital work will be written. All of it will require that you be able to set down your thoughts, suggestions, goals on paper – so clearly and so persuasively that those papers serve as your best salesmen.

Therefore, the ability to write well is equally as important to you as the ability to speak well. You must be as fluid with your pen as you are with your tongue. You must be just as much at home writing a technical report as you are telling a friend about a ball game.

You must develop ease in writing.

Ease in writing, and precision in writing, come from two sources, both of which area available to you.

1. Practice and
2. Planning

It is the combination of these two that constitute power writing. Let us see how you can build both of them into your every written word, and HOW YOU CAN DISCOVER EXACXTLY WHAT TO WRITE FROM THE BEGINNING TO THE END OF EVERY PAPER.

Like reading, and perhaps even more so, writing demands a plan of attack, a definite goal that you want to achieve in every composition, and a definite plan to get there. A series of questions that points you immediately on the right road, and keeps you there from the first word you write to the last.

Let's look at such a series of direction questions right now. Let's work out a typical idea – for example, a paper you might prepare for a magazine article, or a speech before your club – and see how these questions with answers avoid errors, strengthen the power of what you have to say and cut your writing time in half.

Let's take as our subject Should America Try to Be First to Land a Man on the Moon? Let's assume that you answer the question with a "Yes," that America should try to land a man on the moon first, and see how you develop the subject.

First of all, you should ask yourself these questions:

What exactly am I going to write about in this paper?

(About whether America should try to be first to land a man on the moon.)

Can I express this key idea in a single sentence, before I begin to write? (Yes. America should be first to land a man on the moon.)

How much am I going to say about it? (I'm going to list the reasons why America should be first.)

What am I NOT going to say about it, because I don't have the room? (Two things: (1) I am not going to list any arguments for the other side, why America should not try to be first; and (2) I am not going to discuss any of the technical problems that we'll have to overcome to reach the moon.)

What specific points am I going to make about this idea? (The specific reasons why we should be first: Because it will help our prestige with the neutral nations. Because it will aid our economy. Because it will yield new inventions that we might otherwise not have discovered. Because it will give us new military strength. And because it fulfills man's destiny to explore the universe, in which America should always be in the forefront.)

How many of these points are there? (Five.)

In what order should they be arranged? Which should come first, second, third, and so on? (In this order: First, military strength; second, neutral nations; third, aid to the economy; fourth, scientific inventions; and fifth, exploration.

Which of these points are the most important; which should be given separate paragraphs? (All of them.)

Which points should I group into one paragraph? (None.)

What is the best way to catch my reader's interest? Probably with strong, emphatic assertion at the very beginning. Something like this: "There are at least five vital reasons why America should be first to put a man on the moon, any one of which would more than justify this project's cost.")

How do I end? Can I think of a good last sentence before I begin to write? (Yes. A summary sentence something like this: "Therefore, to keep our, military strength from falling behind, to maintain our prestige with uncommitted nations of the world, to strengthen our own economy, to receive the benefits from otherwise overlooked scientific discoveries, and to assure America's leadership at the forefront of human destiny, it is essential that this country be the first nation to place a man on the moon.")

HOW YOU PERFECT YOUR COMPOSITION BEFORE YOU BEGIN TO WRITE IT

The question outlined above give you two major benefits. They force you to chose a definite, easily handled topic, clearly formulated, concrete and specific, with no chance of wandering over its chosen limits. And they help you write about this topic one step at a time, with each step in its proper place.

Without such a blueprint, you simply won't know where you're going, and revising your paper will take you more time than originally writing it.

Now, once you have the answers to these questions, arrange them quickly in a Main Thought Outline, just as you do in your daily reading. The process in both reading and writing is the same, but it is done in the reverse. In writing, you get main thoughts first, build them into an outline second, and then write the paper itself on the basis of that outline.

Here is how you build that outline.

Write your title for the paper across the top of the outline. "Why America Should Be First to Put a Man on the Moon."

Write the first sentence directly below this title: "There are at least five vital reasons why America should be the first to put a man on the moon, any one of which would more than justify this project's cost."

Take the first major idea and mark it with Roman numeral I:

"I. To keep our military strength from falling behind."

If this first major idea demands more than one paragraph to explain it fully, then mark each one of these paragraphs with the capital letters A, B, C, and so on:

128

"A. To keep our missile strength from falling behind."

"B. To keep our missile-guidance strength from falling behind."

"C. To keep our military technology from falling behind."

Each of these paragraphs will have several sentences within it, to develop important details. These detail sentences are marked in the outline by Arabic numerals, and are placed under the capital letter paragraphed to which they belong. For example, in paragraph A above, you would have these detail sentences:

"A. To keep our missile strength from falling behind."

1. Will force us to develop larger and larger rockets.
2. More powerful engines.
3. Longer ranges.
4. And therefore heavier payloads.

Continue on, developing every major idea in this way, marking them with the Roman numerals II, III, IV, and so on. Then breaking them into their separate paragraphs, and marking them into their separate paragraphs, and marking these with the capital letters, A,B,C, and so on. Then outlining the individual detail – sentences with Arabic numerals 1,2,3 and so on, till you have finished outlining the entire paper.

You then write in your concluding sentence, and you are finished with the outline. Here is a brief sample of what that outline will look like at that stage:

WHY AMERICA SHOULD BE FIRST TO PUT A MAN ON THE MOON

There are at least five vital reasons why America should be the first to put a man on the moon, any of which would more than justify this project's cost:

I.

A. 1. 2. 3. 4.
B. 1. 2. 3.
C. 1. 2. 3. 4.

II.

To keep our military strength from falling behind.

To keep our missile strength from falling behind. Will force us to develop larger and larger rockets. More powerful engines. Longer ranges.

And therefore heavier payloads.

To keep our missile-guidance strength from falling behind. Better radar. More sophisticated computers. Satellite tracking stations.

To keep our military technology from falling behind. Research facilities. Manufacturing plants. Testing and feedback.

Space education.

To maintain our prestige with the uncommitted nations of the world.

A. And so on, till the outline is finished.

To prevent a Russian "reign of terror."

HOW TO WRITE THE FINISHED DRAFT OF THE PAPER

From this point on, the final draft of the composition writes itself.

You take the title and the first sentence and put them down on the paper. Then take main idea I and phrase it into your next paragraph, like this:

"First of all, of course, such a project is necessary to keep our military strength from falling behind that of the Soviet Union.

Now take each of the three paragraphs under this main idea I, and build them according to the outline, like this:

In our comparative missile strength alone, the moon project will yield vast benefits. It will force us to develop larger rockets. It will force us to devise larger engines to propel them. These larger engines will give us longer ranges for all our missiles, space and military. And they will result in heavier payloads, wherever we have to deliver them.

The same exact benefits will be felt in our missile-guidance program. From moon project research, we will gain better radar. We will develop more sophisticated computer systems, with faster speeds and greater accuracy. And we may even find ourselves with a network of satellite tracking stations spread across the globe.

And so on. Paragraph by paragraph, right through the entire paper.

When you are through, you will have a composition that develops your subject thoroughly, that presents your points in logical, persuasive order that makes good reading and makes sense, and that persuades other people tom your point of view.

TIPS ON WRITING THAT DEVELOP CLARITY AND POWER

1. Every paragraph should contain one main idea and the details that develop it. When you go on to discuss a second main idea, start a new paragraph.

This has been shown over and over again in the examples we have given above.

2. Each sentence, in its turn, should contain only one idea. The great mistake most poor writers make is in trying to crowd too many ideas into a single sentence. This results in huge, clumsy, poorly understood sentences. When you get to a second idea – or when you find two or more ideas crowded against each other in a single sentence – separate them and build each into its own sentence.

EXAMPLE:

WRONG WAY: After we arrived home from the trip, tired and dirty, we immediately went upstairs, where we unpacked our clothes and hung them up, before we allowed ourselves to take a shower and go to bed.

CLEARER AND MORE POWERFUL: We arrived home from the trip, tired and dirty. We immediately went upstairs. Yet, before we allowed ourselves to take a shower and go to bed, we unpacked our clothes and hung them up.

3. Long sentences are usually confused sentences. One sure way to avoid this mistake, and to write clearer, stronger sentences, is to keep the subject and predicate of each sentence as close together as possible.

EXAMPLE:

WRONG WAY: The man whom Tom had seen earlier that day running away from the bank spun around when he saw Tom.

The subject of this sentence is "man" and its predicate is "spun". The reason the sentence is confusing is that this subject and predicate are separated so widely by the clause "whom Tom had seen earlier that day running away from the bank." Therefore, to make these two thoughts far more powerful and clear, they should be separated like this:

RIGHT WAY: It was the man whom Tom had seen earlier that day running away the bank. When he saw Tom again, he spun around.

4. Make sure your sentences are connected correctly. You have to point out the relation between one sentence and the next. Otherwise, your reader won't know where your train of thought is going.

Connecting words are and, yet, but, so, or, for, however, therefore, thus, otherwise, because, from, such, this and so on. They point out to your reader what your second sentence has to do with your first, what your third has to do with your second, and so on.

EXAMPLES: A good exercise would be to go through a few pages of any good book and underline the connecting words the author uses. Ask yourself how each connection word ties in one sentence with the sentence that goes before.

This way, you will develop skill in using these tie-in words, and your papers will be a powerful procession of closely woven thoughts.

IN SUMMARY:

The ability to write well is as important as the ability to speak well, and it is as easy to learn.

You should learn and practice the principles of planning from today on. Before you start to write a word you should already have defined your subject, your main thoughts, and your opening and closing sentences.

And you should have arranged them in paragraph order in a Main Thought Outline, so your paper will practically write itself when you sit down to begin it.

PART FOUR
Mastering facts – the art of remembering and review

CHAPTER 14
Errors – the royal road to knowledge

Every person, no matter how bright or slow he is, learns some facts quickly and has trouble with others.

Those he learns easily require little outside help. It is the troublesome fact, the error-causing fact, the fact that blocks the road to understanding that we must concentrate upon.

The telltale symptom of trouble, of course, is a mistake in your work. Most people are troubled by such mistakes. They do not realize that if they are handled correctly, they are worth their weight in gold.

Why? Because a mistake is actually nothing more or less than a signpost in your work that identifies misunderstanding.

And by analyzing what went wrong in each of those mistakes, and correcting it, you will achieve a far deeper level of understanding and competence than you could ever gain without them.

This is perfectly in accord with prime rule of all self-improvement – work on weaknesses. Your strengths you will always have. But your weaknesses must be identified and gone over and over again until they are no longer there.

Let us therefore examine this technique of turning a mistake into gold. It is as simple this:

HOW YOU CAN PROFIT FROM YOUR MISTAKES

It is never enough for you simply to glance at a test when it is handed back to you and notice that you have made an error on it.

For every test error (or any error on any work) that you make, you must be able to answer these three questions about that error before you go on to new work:

1. Where in the problem did you make the mistake?
2. What did you do wrong that caused you to make that mistake?
3. What is the correct operation that will avoid that same kind of mistake in the future?

Let's see how these three questions turn errors into accomplishments.

STEP ONE: LOCATE THE ERROR

For example, let's say that you come up with a wrong answer in a profit and loss problem.

You know that the answer is wrong, but where exactly did it go wrong?

Was it a mistake in multiplication or subtractions, or addition inside the problem?

Was it only one mistake or several?

To find out, break the problem down into steps. Check each step to find out which one went wrong. Don't rest till you can pinpoint the exact step where each error occurred.

STEP TWO: FIND OUT WHAT CAUSED IT:

Now, when you've located the exact spot where the error occurred, you have to identify its cause.

Let's say that it was a mistake in one of your percentages. You took a 47% mark-up on $500 worth of goods, and came up with a sales price of $745.

What caused you to make this mistake?

Was it simply carelessness? Or is that mistake a warning that you're weak in your multiplication?

STEP THREE: CORRECT THE CAUSE OF THE ERROR

If it was carelessness, review again the techniques of checking an answer to make sure its right.

If, however, you do show a weakness in multiplication, stop everything and review multiplication. Do it over and over again until it becomes automatic and automatically right.

Remember, you have to correct the cause of an error before you can permanently correct the error itself. If you do not correct the cause first, the error will simply repeat itself later on.

STEP FOUR: CORRECT THE ERROR ITSELF

Now take a fresh sheet of paper. Copy the problem onto that paper and work it again.

This time it should come out right. If it does, file it away and come back to it the following week. Try it again on a fresh piece of paper.

If you get it right again, then you can forget about it. If not, do it again. Never allow yourself to make the same mistake twice!

138

STEP FIVE: DO SIMILAR PROBLEMS TO MAKE SURE YOU'VE GOT THE CORRECT TECHNIQUE

At the same time, give yourself several other mark-up problems. Concentrate on them. Within a short time you'll have mastered them all, and the correct answers will flow from your pen, with perfect confidence.

IN SUMMARY: Follow this same technique with every mistake you make.

Break the problem down into steps. See which step went wrong. Find out why. Correct the cause of the error. Work the problem the right way. And keep doing it over and over again until the right answer is absolutely automatic.

This way mistakes help rather than harm you. You won't make that mistake – or its first cousin – again. You have removed a misunderstanding-roadblock from your mind.

This process of turning errors into achievements is one of the finest forms of review. We now turn to a complete discussion of this all- important subject.

CHAPTER 15
How to burn facts, lessons, whole subjects into your mind – for good

We are now ready to review what you have learned so far in this book, and tie it together into one over-all plan for mastering any subject you may study.

Mastering a course – any course – consists of the following logical steps:

1. Find out what it is that you have to learn in each assignment in the course.
2. Read the assignment to get at the heart of its meaning.
3. Write that core meaning down in your notebook in a few brief sentences or phrases, related to each other through the outline form.
4. Tie the outline of that assignment into the assignment that came before it.
5. Then review as much as you have studied of the entire book or course EVERY WEEK, to get an over-all view of everything you've learned.
6. At the end of the term, a week or two before the final test, make a final review of your strengths and weaknesses throughout the entire course. Here you find out what you know well; what you should know better; what you really do not know at all.

And on the basis of this final review, you create the final study schedule for the week before the test.

This, then, is your Plan of Mastery for your studies.

We have already discussed Step 1 through 4. We now turn to Steps 5 and 6 – the strategy of review, of fixing the heart of your course permanently in your mind.

WHAT REVIEW IS NOT

First of all, let us define review by saying quite definitely what it is not.

Review is not cramming, not last-minute effort, not the desperate piling up of information in frenzied disorder.

This type of cramming always fails. It always has failed. It always will fail.

Why? Because it attempts to store up large quantities of unorganized material. And without organization. There can be no memory. Material crammed into your brain leaks out again as fast as it goes in.

WHAT IS EFFECTIVE REVIEW?

Boiled down to its essentials, active effective reviewing is nothing more or less than this:

Continuous self-examination – of the essential parts of a course.

Effective review, then, consists of these two essential steps:

1. Boiling down the material of the course to its essentials, and then boiling the essentials down again and again and again, till you've mastered every word of the core meaning of that course.
2. Periodically reviewing that core material – through continuous self-examination – till every word of its content is right at the tip of your tongue, ready to be instantly formed into an answer. For example, mathematics is thus reduced to rules, definitions, types of problems that will be encountered in the final test, and the formulas and procedures that will solve them. Then all this essential knowledge is rehearsed, over and over again, till the correct answer to any one of the problems an automatic and instant reaction.

This is the same combination of knowledge and practice that makes a champion line backer, a top-flight golfer, or a superbly successful executive.

Once you have reviewed your course in this way – in other words, once you have reduced it to its essentials and practiced quizzing yourself on those essentials till they have become second nature – you are ready to breeze through any test that can be thrown at you on that subject.

Now, let's examine this process of review and readiness, step by step. There are three steps:

1. Weekly review.
2. Final organization of notebook. 3. Final quiz-review of the entire course. Let's look at each one:

STEP ONE: THE WEEKLY REVIEW

Effective review, of course, is not a once-a-course activity. It goes on constantly, first as part of your day-by-day study, then to survey a larger area once every week, and then to insure understanding of the entire course at the end of the term.

We have already discussed, in Chapter 9, the first step in this continuous process. We went over the three questions you use to tie in each new chapter with the one that went before. These were:

"In one sentence, what did I learn from last night's chapter?" "How does this tie in with the chapter before?" "What questions will I be asked on it in next week's test?

Now, at the end of each study week, you go one step further. Each week, you set aside one additional half hour for review of the entire book up to that point.

During this hour, you review each chapter outline in your notebook. You then tie them together – in a continuously growing over- all view of the book as a whole – with this series of questions and answers:

"How many chapters have I now read in this book?" (Using the history book as our example: Three, plus an introduction.)

"What is the title of the book?" (A History of Civilization.)

"Does this title give the theme of the book?" (It does.) If it did not, you would then ask the question:

"What is the theme of the book?" (A history of civilization.)

"What, in one sentence, is the core meaning of the introduction?" (A study of history keeps us from making the same mistakes all over again that our ancestors made.)

"What is the title of the first chapter?" ("The First Men.")

"What, in one sentence, is the core meaning of the first chapter?" (Primitive man spent almost all his time getting enough food to keep alive, until he invented agriculture.)

"What is the title of the second chapter?" ("The Near East.")

"What, in our sentence, is the core meaning of the second chapter?" (The first great civilizations in history – ruled by kings and priests and resting on slavery – were built in the Near East.)

"How does the second chapter tie in with the first?" (By showing the tremendous growth in civilization agriculture made possible, even though this civilization was enjoyed only by the few who had seized rule.)

"What is the title of the third chapter? ("The Greeks.")

"What, in one sentence, is the core meaning of the third chapter?" (The Greeks developed the first Western civilization, inventing democracy, science, philosophy, literature, and so on.)

"How does the third chapter tie in with the second?"

(By showing the contrast between the older, king-and-priest-dominated civilizations of the Near East, and the new freedom that characterized Greek civilization.)

And so on.

Chapter by chapter, every week of each course.

This never-ceasing weekly review pays off several ways. It keeps the older chapters fresh in your mind. It ties in each new chapter with all the material that preceded it.

It give you an ever-growing over-all view of the course as a unified whole. It cuts down the amount of reviewing you will need to do it in the last two weeks before your final exams.

And it helps you to simplify and to bring your notebook up to date, like this:

STEP TWO: THE FINAL ORGANIZATION OF YOUR NOTEBOOK

At the end course, when you are ready to begin your final review, you have in your notebook:

1. A main-thought outline of every textbook chapter in the course.
2. A main-thought outline of every lecture you have been given in the course.
3. If there are any, main-thought outlines of any outside reference reading you have been assigned during the course, done in the same way as any daily reading assignment.
4. A fundamental vocabulary page for the course as a whole.
5. A list of the mistakes you have made in your test papers during the progress of the course.

These five different parts of your notebook must now be brought together into a single final outline page for each chapter in the course.

They must be blended together – unified – with all the duplicate facts removed. They must arranged in a single, logical order, so that every fact you have learned during the

entire course fits in perfectly, and can be remembered –
automatically – the instant you need it.

This final blending is done in this way:

FIRST:

For each chapter, take your reading notes and lecture notes
(and, if there are any, outside reference notes) and lay them
side by side.

Then take a third sheet of paper and start to blend them in,
point by point. Start with the chapter title, then the first main
thought underneath that title, then the second, and right on
down the line.

To help you with this blending task ask yourself the following
questions:

"Is this fact repeated by both sources?" If so, throw it out.

"Is this fact new?" If so, put it under the proper heading in your
revised outline.

"Do I have to change the order of my headings because of any
new facts?" Sometimes when material from separate sources is
put together, you will find that neither of the separate sources is
put together, you will find that neither of the older outlines can
contain the blended facts. In this case, you must construct a
brand-new outline and order containing all the new facts in
their proper relation to each other.

"Are all these facts really important – are they really main
thoughts – or are some of them merely details describing other
main thoughts already picked up from another source?" If so,
leave them out.

146

These questions cause you to weigh and choose and reject. They make your mind work. In themselves, they are an excellent form of review. And when you are finished answering them, and shaping their answers into a final main thought chapter outline, you will pretty well know everything there is to know about the material in that chapter.

SECOND:

Now, go back over your lecture notes for that chapter, and ask yourself the following questions:

"What questions will I be most likely asked about this chapter?"

"What points have been stressed in classroom lectures?"

"What information were we told to pay special attention to in the textbook?"

Every time you find the answer to one of these questions in your lecture notes, place a red check in front of that point in your revised main-thought outline. This check will serve as a signal to you when you compose your final review questions, as we will describe below.

Now throw away your reading notes, lecture notes, and reference notes.

You have no more need for them, since they have been blended into your revised main-thought outlines.

THIRD:

Now turn to the fundamental-vocabulary page. Remove this page from your notebook and lay it alongside your revised main-thought outline for the course.

Go down the vocabulary, word by word, and check off the point in the main-thought outlines where that word is first used in the course. At that point, make an asterisk (*) in the main-thought outline, and then write the word and its definition at the bottom of that outline page.

Do this till you have exhausted every word you have in the fundamental vocabulary. You have then tied the vocabulary in with your notes, and gained a deeper understanding of both in doing it.

But do not throw away the fundamental-vocabulary page. Continue to carry it at the back of the notebook as an instant reference if you should forget the meaning of the words as they appear in more advanced lessons.

FOURTH:

Now take out your daily or weekly written work, and check each one

of the mistakes you have made during the entire course.

Wherever you have made a mistake, place a red check mark against the same point in your main-thought outlines. This again reminds you to pay special attention to that point in your final review.

You now have a completely revised and ready-for-review notebook. It contains every fact you have learned from your reading, your lectures and your reference research, all blended together into one thoroughly understood stream of thought.

In addition, you have incorporated into those outlines probable test questions, a thorough understanding of the vocabulary of the course, and review signals for every weak spot that has shown up in your work for the entire term.

You are now ready to perform one final review operation on that notebook, which will thoroughly prepare you for your final test by enabling you to anticipate 80 per cent or more of all the questions your teacher can give you, IN THE EXACT FORM THAT TEACHER CAN PHRASE THEM.

STEP THREE: THE FINAL QUIZ-REVIEW OF THE ENTIRE COURSE

Let us say that you have begun your final revision of your notebook two weeks before the final exam. It has taken you one week to complete this revision, and thus to master the main thoughts of the entire course.

You now have one week left to prepare yourself to breeze through that final exam. In the next chapter we will outline day-by-day, step-by-step

procedures for that final week. Right now, however, we will see how you take your revised notes during that final week, and turn them into your own private test before the real test, to make sure you know every detail of that material.

There are two reasons, of course, why you take this private test before the real test:

1. Obviously, because it gives you one final chance to again review your material, to gain still deeper understanding of it, and more confidence in handling it.
2. Because it is one thing to know the core material of a course, and quite another thing to be able quickly and accurately to answer test questions about it. To really whiz thought a test, you should be familiar with questions you are going to be asked on that test – not only their form, but their very content. And the only way can discover that content – outside of cheating – is to construct your own test out of the same materials your teacher will use it construct his.

Therefore you now begin to turn your revised notes into test questions, in this way:

HOW TO MAKE UP YOUR OWN TEST QUESTIONS

As we mentioned In Chapter 9, each page of your notes is written on one side only. You have purposely left the opposite of those notes blank. You are now going to put that blank side to work.

Let us say that you are going to review our sample chapter 3, The Five Roads to Cost Reduction. You have already revised your outline notes, to include both text and lecture ideas into one over-all outline.

You now turn that sheet of paper over and write across the top of the blank side: The Five Roads to Cost Reduction – Test Questions.

You are now ready to make up your questions. In doing this you must remember that, in your final exam, you will be given two general types of questions.

First, the Short-Answer questions, such as multiple choice, true-false, fill-in, and so on.

Second, the Essay questions, which ask you to write a paragraph or more in answer to every question.

In order to prepare for both types of questions, you draw a horizontal line across the middle of your paper, dividing it in two.

At the top left – hand corner of the upper half, right under the over-all title, write: Short-Answer Questions:

And at the top left-hand corner of the lower half, right under your dividing line, write: Essay Questions:

Now draw a vertical line down the middle of the paper, to divide your questions from your answers. Your paper now looks like this:

Five Roads To Cost Reduction – Test Questions

Short – Answer Questions

| Answers

_____ _____

| 1. | 2. | 3. | 4. | etc.... | |

_____|_____ |

Essay Questions 1. | 2. | 3. | 4. | etc... |

| |

You are now ready to compose your questions. HOW TO MAKE UP SHORT-ANSWER QUESTIONS

| Answers

In a later Chapter, you will be shown each of the different types of short-answer questions, along with simple formulas to greatly aid you in answering them.

Here we can touch on only a few of these types of questions, to use as examples of how you should convert your lectures notes into a final self-quiz. You proceed in this way:

First, of course, you take every point that your teacher has emphasized in his lectures, and convert it into a test question.

Let's say, for example, that your teacher has stressed the methods of cutting capital equipment costs in his lecture. Immediately construct a cross-out test question on his point, and use it as the first short-answer question on the page, like this:

Which of the following four procedures is NOT a way to cut capital equipment costs?

- Reducing costs of depreciation, replacement, maintenance, and interest.
- Holding down inventories.
- Operations research.
- Sharpening accounting procedures.

The answer, of course, is c. But do not yet write in that answer. Instead, go on to the next question.

This next series of questions revolves around those points that you have made errors on in previous work. For each error you have made, you now compose a self-test question.

For example, let's say you had difficulty before in remembering the various ways to cut raw-material costs. You now, therefore, construct a true-false question on just this point, in this way:

TRUE OR FALSE: Three good ways to cut raw material coats are precise purchasing specifications, inspection of incoming materials, and financial control of sources.

The answer, of course, is true. And so you go down the entire list of important points, constructing a different question for every one of the types mentioned later in the book. In this way, you become thoroughly familiar with each one of these question types, as they apply to the material you will be tested on.

You even use the same procedure to make sure you know the exact meaning of each of the words in your fundamental vocabulary. For example, suppose you want to be absolutely certain of the meaning of Operations Research. To test yourself on this point, construct the following question:

OPERATIONS RESEARCH means most nearly: a) Cost Accounting; b) Statistical Decision Making; C) Computer Planning; d) Time and Motion Study.

The answer is c. But the construction of such a question forces you to think deeply about the meaning of this new word, to compare and contrast it with the other new terms you have learned in this course, and to dig deeper into more and more profitable levels of understanding.

HOW TO MAKE UP ESSAY QUESTIONS

The same procedure holds true on preparing your Essay Questions. First go over the important points stressed by your teacher. Then the points you have been confused on before. Then whatever other ideas you believe that you will be tested on in your final exam.

For example, on manufacturing costs, a simple essay type questions would be this:

List five ways to cut manufacturing costs.

Or, as a more complicated essay-type question:

You have just been appointed sales manager of the ABC Company Describe five ways that you would attempt to cut their sales costs, in order, and tell why you think each if these ways would be effective.

HOW TO ANSWER ESSAY-TYPE QUESTIONS ON YOUR SELF- QUIZ PAPER

When you have written all your questions – both short answer and essay type- down the left-hand side of your paper, you are ready to take your own quiz and write the answers.

You do not do this the same day that you composed the questions. Wait a day, and then come back to the quiz.

Without looking at your notes, write the answer completely. For the essay-type questions, however, do not write a complete answer. Instead, outline as you would do in a actual test.

You are only trying to develop the main ideas for your answer, and the order in which you would arrange them. Once you have this, you can be satisfied, and go on to the next question.

For example, in the essay question two, about the sales manger position described on the last page, you would outline your answer in this way:

Way To Cut Cost

1. Advertising
2. Warehousing
3. Transportation
4. New Specialists

Reason Why

1. Biggest cost today
2. Greatest per-cent improvement
3. Big waste in most co's
4. May be cut entirely

HOW TO REVIEW YOUR SELF-QUIZZES

Once you have taken the test, you grade yourself right or wrong, just as your teacher would. Those answers that you have right you forget until the last day before the test.

Those answers that you have wrong you review again the next day, in this way:

Place a red check mark in front of the question you have missed. The next day, take out the self-quiz again, cover the answer with a sheet of fresh paper, and try to answer the question again.

If you get it correctly this second time, forget it till the last day before the test.

If you miss it again, reread your notes, and then turn back to the original textbook material and reread it again. If you still do not understand it after this rereading immediately speak to your teacher about it, going over it with him until you are absolutely sure of it.

Remember your goal is to make certain that you understand every important idea in the course well enough to allow you to answer any questions on it that can be thrown at you. You can accept nothing less.

WHAT THESE SELF-QUIZZES WILL DO FOR YOU

If you have done them correctly, when you are through with these self-quizzes, you have accomplished the dream of every person who has ever walked down a classroom aisle to take a final exam:

You will actually know the examination question in advance!

You see, you teacher, in preparing his final tests, his no more material to choose from than you. Both you and your teacher will have to concentrate on the same broad ideas and important details as the sources for your test material.

Therefore, to a surprisingly large extent, you both must come up with exactly the same questions.

Think of the thrill you will get when you march into the final exam and find dozens of the same exact test questions waiting there for you – with the correct answers perfectly stored away in your head, ready to spring onto the paper.

Think of the head start this will give you over more poorly prepared classmates. Think of the tremendous burst of confidence this will raise in you – to completely erase any nervousness you might have brought into the room with you, carry you through every question on the test, with your mind already revved up to full working power, pulling out correct answers as fast as you can write them down on the page.

Isn't this a wonderful gift to give yourself, for only a few disciplined minutes each day, the final week before you take that test?

IN SUMMARY:

A truly effective review is continuous self-examination of the essential parts of a course.

This continuous self-examination goes on every week of the course, right up until the final examination. It takes place in three stages:

1. The weekly review. Where you tie in every new chapter you have learned during the week with all the material that has gone before it. In this way you gain a constantly growing over-all view of the course, with all its important parts fresh in your mind.
2. The final organization of your notebook. Where you organize and blend in all the information you have received during the course – from your textbook, lectures, outside reference work, vocabulary building, and your error feedback. From this blending, you gain a final unified outline of the backbone ideas of the course, all at you're your fingertips for instant reference.
3. The final quiz-review of the entire course. Where you write your own final exam on the important ideas you have learned in the entire term, becoming familiar and at ease with both the content and form of such an exam. From this final self-quiz you gain dozens of the actual questions that will asked of you in your final exam, plus the confidence that you can answer any other question that can be asked of you.

With this solid bedrock foundation of review to back you, we now turn to the final examinations themselves, and see dozens of simple ways to improve your performance in them.

PART SIX
How to breeze though test

CHAPTER 16
The week before the test – what to do and what not to do

The final goal of all your planning – all your work, learning and relearning and review – is one or two or three hours in a closed room, proving your accomplishment, in the educational ritual called the test, which separates the winners from the losers.

Some people object to tests as unfair, anxiety causing, and not really proving anything. This is untrue. Life is a series of tests. Some are written, some are verbal, some are economic or social or moral.

In any case, you had better get used to passing all of them now. The winner's circle is an entirely different world from the habitat of the also-ran.

THE FIRST GREAT STEP IN IMPROVING ANYONE'S TEST GRADES

Test performance can be improved, just as performance in any competitive activity can be improved. And as in developing any other skill, the two magic ingredients are:

1. Knowledge, and 2. Practice.

And as in any other form of pay-off competition, there is always one great enemy to face and overcome: fear.

Fear destroys people in tests, just as fear can destroy people in business or social life. The person who tenses up, panics, loses all his carefully stored information the moment he faces the test paper, is beaten before he even tries.

Therefore the first step in preparing yourself to master any kind of examination is to always ask this question:

What causes fear in a test situation? The answer is twofold:

1. Not knowing the material upon which you will be tested. 2. Not knowing the forms and procedures by which you will be tested.

Either one of these two test fears can knock you right out of a top grade. They can cause a performance 30 per cent to 50 per cent less than you are really capable of giving.

You must prevent this loss. But how?

Quite simply, really, in these three tested and proved ways:

1. Preparation.
2. Familiarity.
3. Practice.

Let's discuss each of them in turn:

First, of course, preparation. Knowing the material of your course. Knowing it backward and forward. Boiling it down into its main ideas; arranging those main ideas in the right logical order so that one automatically suggests another; and filing those ideas away in your mind so permanently that they spring to your tongue or hand the very instant you need them.

This preparation for the final exam begins the very first day you open your book. This book has been a step-by-step blueprint on how to conduct that preparation, how to make it as thorough as possible, and how to make it instantly available again, at the moment of pay-off.

FAMILIARITY BREEDS CONTEMPT – WITH TESTS AS WELL AS PEOPLE

Second, after you have mastered the content of your course, you must then equally master the forms by which you will be questioned about it.

Tests rattle people by their very appearance. The sight of a strange new way to ask a question can cause a person to miss an answer that he knows perfectly well. Questions, as every student knows, can be tricky. Your job is to take the trickery out of them before you encounter them in the test room.

This demands that you sit down and learn, one by one, the types of questions you will be asked in your exams. You learn how

these questions are built, how to read them, what you must do to solve them, and how they themselves can help you solve them.

Then you go over the same type of question two, three, four or more times, until you are as familiar with way to work out the answer to that question, as you are with the way to write your own name.

Your goal is simple. You must make absolutely certain that you are never confronted with a type or form of question that you have never seen before.

The moment you glance at that question, its form must be so familiar to you that you know automatically, without a second thought, the procedure by which you will answer it. You must be able to concentrate instantly on the content of that question, to devote your full energies to retrieving of that question a second thought.

This is what the next two chapters will do for you. First, they will give you every type of short-answer question now in popular use. Then every type of essay question.

They will build into your test-taking personality familiarity – your second great weapon against fear.

PRACTICE MAKES PERFECT – PERFECT KNOWLEDGE, PERFECT CONFIDENCE

Third, and finally, once you know the course material, and once you know the form or type of questions you're going to be asked about it, then you out the two together in constant, continuous practice.

With the system we have taught you in these pages you will actually be taking tests from the very first day you open a new book. You will test yourself every single night in your nightly review, with every tie- in talk you have each morning, every weekly review you finish each Friday.

Every time you do a problem in mathematics, you test yourself. Every time you correct an error in your homework you retest yourself.

Every day, you subject yourself to a barrage of questions. Till questions become second nature to you. Till you can smell a possible test question on a printed page a mile away. Till your mind becomes one great razor-sharp instrument for asking and answering questions. And, at that moment, you can take credit not only for top grades you will get in these tests, but for having developed a truly educated mind.

Education is, in the last analysis, the ability to ask and answer questions. It is active knowledge seeking out new knowledge to deepen its understanding. It is thought in action, able to learn, to solve, to build.

YOUR STUDY FOR THE FINAL TWO WEEKS BEFORE THE TEST

This continuous question-and-answer approach to education keeps you constantly reviewing, constantly prepared for whatever tests you may encounter. Therefore, as we have seen in the previous chapter, formal preparation for your final test requires much less time than that needed by your less-organized classmates.

Once again, however, for these final two weeks, you draw up a definite plan of attack. To get the greatest benefit out of every study hour, for every course, do this:

1. Divide up the last two weeks before the final test into six working days. Then decide how many hours you will have in each working day to devote to study – let us say three hours a day. This gives you eighteen working hours per week for the last two weeks.
2. You then take the number of courses you will have to study for. Let us say there are four. Thus four courses into eighteen hours each week gives you four-hours-plus during the week to devote to each course.
3. During the first week, your review will consist of rewriting and blending your notes. Let us assume that you spend all your allotted four hours per course in that first week, on this active rewriting of your notes.
4. During the final week, devote your first two hours to writing your own final exam about those notes.

You can devote the third hour – a day later – to taking this elf-exam, checking your weak points, reviewing the material that will deepen your understanding of them, and marking each still-troublesome idea for one last review the next day.

FINAL HOUR OF PREPARATION – PREFERABLY WITH A FRIEND

You are now ready for your last self-exam. You will take it on this basis:

What you have done up to this point has been a process of condensation, of boiling down the material of each course in two ways:

First, to its main thoughts, its backbone meaning, its important ideas that you must be tested upon.

Second, to each one of these main ideas that is particularly hard for you. That you do not quite understand. That you cannot answer as quickly and accurately as you can all the others.

Throughout your hours of self-examination, you have gradually mastered and pout aside those important ideas that you thoroughly understand. In your two weeks of the final review, you first refreshed your memory on these well-known facts, and then tested your ability to recall them easily and completely.

Now put aside. You know that you can answer any test question about them.

This leaves you, in this last hour of review, face to face with your own particular trouble-makers.

These are the facts upon which you are vague. The problems you cannot solve automatically. The questions that might trip you up without this one final hour of mastery.

Now you attack them directly, in every form, shape, and way that you can think of.

If possible, you should have some other member of the family with you in this final hour of mastery. Their job here is that of question-asker.

They should take every one of those trouble-makers in turn, and invent five, six, seven different approaches, different questions to sharpen your mind about them.

For example, they might take the final trouble-maker, and first ask a true-false question about it. Then switch to a multiple-answer question. Then to cross-out question. Then to a comparison-contrast question.

Let them ask as many questions as they think up about that one trouble-maker. And keep asking till the right answer becomes automatic on your lips. Then go on to the next trouble-maker and do the same.

Of course, familiarity with the subject matter will greatly aid this final, intensive quiz. Therefore, for at least this last hour, it is advisable that you review this material with another person who is attending the same class, or taking the same course.

Let us assume that both have prepared your own final exams in approximately the same way described above. In this case you both have prepared your own self-quiz on the same material.

But no two minds think alike, and one may have picked some vital point that the other has neglected. Therefore, for the first half hour of this last review hour, let each of you give the other his own quiz.

This should be done orally. Fast. With the answers springing from your lips almost the instant the questions are finished.

Many of the questions you will have already anticipated, phrased almost exactly the same. Realizing this will give your confidence a huge boost.

Other questions will be slight rephrases, or on different points than you might have stressed. This will give you a chance to pull the material out of your mind, to become accustomed to turning questions into answers automatically.

When the quizzes are over, each of you then turns to his own trouble-makers. You intensively quiz each other on just these points. Discuss your answers. The two points of view merge. New insights are gained by both of you.

This may be the final push that leads you to absolute understanding of a point that has been bothering you since the beginning of the course, so you can now file it away and forget it.

HOW TO MAKE SURE YOU REMEMBER YOUR MEMORY WORK WHEN YOU GO INTO THE EXAMINATION ROOM

In addition to this backbone meaning of your course, you will be confronted from time to time with other facts, equally as important, which you must memorize exactly, detail for detail. These may be mathematical formulas, history dates, equations in chemistry or physics, and so on.

With such facts, your problem is one of sheer memorization. You must have them engraved on your memory by the time you walk into the exam room. You can do this most easily by following the following procedure:

1. Buy a packet of 5 1/2 by 8-inch library cards that fit into your pocket. Each formula you want to memorize you write down exactly on one of these cards. Use a separate card for each formula you wish to retain.
2. On the front of each card write down the name of the formula. For example, you might write on the front of one card: To find the area of a circle.
3. $A=R^2$

On the back of the card, write the formula itself. For example:

4. Carry these cards with you for a few days. Whenever you have a spare moment, pull them out, look at the identifying name on the front and try to recite the exact formula from memory. Then turn the card over to see if you are correct.
5. When you have repeated the corrected formula three times from memory, take the card and file it away till the week before the final test. If you cannot repeat it three times from memory, continue in this way:
6. The final week before the test, each night take each of the difficult formulas and lay them in a pile, face up on your study table. Read their names one by one, and then write down their formulas on a piece of paper. Then check your answers against the backs of your cards.
7. Right or wrong, continue this writing and checking procedure for five nights before the final test.
8. On the day of the test, in the morning before you leave your home, run through the hardest of the cards again – writing and then checking, and if necessary, correcting.
9. Then take these hard-formula cards with you to the test. When you reach the test room, one minute before the test begins, take out the cards again. Take them one by one, and this time write the formula down on the face of the card, underneath the name.

168

10. Then check the back of the card to see if you are right. If you are right, underline the correct formula on the front of the card. If you arte wrong, write down the correct formula on the front of the card. If you are wrong, write down the correct formula on the front of the card once more.
11. Then tear up the cards and throw them away. Walk directly to your desk, take the exam paper as soon as it is given to you and write the correct formulas in its margin.

You now have the correct formulas at your fingertips, ready to go to work for you in the examination.

THE NIGHT BEFORE THE TEST One last note on this final week before the test. We have tried to prepare you as perfectly as humanly possible for this examination. We

therefore assume that you are ready to take this final exam – as only one of a series of examinations that you have been taking all year long – the day before the test.

Therefore any final study the night before the test would only be wasted effort. Relax that night. A good dinner, perhaps an early movie, then a sound night's sleep.

You will forget nothing in that final night's relaxation. You are prepared. You can take the test the next morning with absolute self- confidence.

IN SUMMARY:

There are three simple secrets to achieving the absolute top grades in any test you will ever take.

1. Preparation – to master the content of the course.
2. Familiarity – with the types of questions that you will be asked.
3. Practice – to combine this content and form into a flawless routine of instant-precision answers.

After a final week of such practice, you should be able to walk into your examination room with complete self-assurance.

To help you do this, we now examine the type of questions you will be asked, and how you can avoid any pitfalls they any present to you.

CHAPTER 17
Types of short-answer tests and how to master them

The most frequent type of test you will encounter is the objective or short-answer or write-in test.

Such tests – and there are at least ten different forms of them – present a series of short questions and then ask you to give a short answer to each. Often this answer is no more than a single word, a yes or a no, or a check mark in the proper space.

Thus these short-answer tests require no writing skill on your part. During the entire test you may not write a single sentence.

Because of this, many people falsely believe that these write-in tests are nothing but measurements of memory, that they do not require you to think, and that the person with the strongest memory is the person who will score the highest on such tests.

Nothing could be further from the truth. A working knowledge of the facts – memorization – is only the first step required to score top marks on such short-answer tests. Assuming that you are thoroughly prepared in the content of the course – as we have tried to achieve in this book – you must also bring to the test at least three other vital skills.

IF YOU WANT TOP GRADES ON THESE OBJECTIVE TESTS, YOU MUST BE ABLE TO:

1. Read with Precision. Short – answer tests are tricky tests. They are designed to expose the sloppy thinker and the careless reader. Time after time, their most heavily graded questions will turn on a single key word.

For example, take this true-false question in American history:

True or false: Many pioneers died in Death Valley where the climate is hot and humid.

This statement is perfectly true right up until the last word, which is false, and which therefore turns the entire statement false. Therefore you must be able to pick out those key words at a glance, understand whether they ask a straight or twisted question, and thus avoid the traps that destroy your unwary classmates.

2. Make Judgments Between Right and Wrong Choices. Most short-answer tests do not merely ask for the right answer to a question; instead they furnish you with a series of possible answers – both right and wrong – to that question.

For example, take this typical question from an English vocabulary test:

Choose the answer which is most nearly OPPOSITE in meaning to the word in capital letters.

1. UNFIT: (A) tight (B) qualified (C) chosen (D) serene (E) necessary.

With such a question, it is equally important to be able to eliminate the wrong answers (tight, chosen, serene, necessary) as it is to be able to select qualified as the right answer.

172

This calls for test judgment. In a moment, we'll show you how to develop it.

2. Reason a Problem, Step by Step, to Its Conclusion And always, of course, in every test, on every question, you must be able to think. To work from the facts that are given to the facts that are asked for.

For example, take this problem from a College Entrance Exam:

Fill in the next two numbers in the following progression: 5 9 13 17 21 25 29 - -

Here you must be able to find a pattern (that each number is 4 higher than the number before it), and project that pattern to come up with the correct answers, 33 and 37.

And you must be able to set up these reasoning patterns, and put them to use, almost as fast as you can run your eyes over the question. We'll show you how in a moment.

So there you have them. The three test abilities you must bring to every examination:

1. The ability to read with precision.
2. The ability to make judgments between right and wrong choices.
3. The ability to reason through a problem.

Now, let's see how we can sharpen each one of those abilities.

Let's turn to the ten most common types of short-answer questions and examine them one by one.

Let's see how some of these questions demand emphasis on one's ability, and other questions require another.

And let's learn the simple techniques that double the power of your abilities on each one of these questions whenever you encounter them on a test.

TYPE OF SHORT-ANSWER QUESTION 1: TRUE-FALSE

DEFINITION: The true-false question is the simplest form of short-answer question. It presents a statement and asks your to tell whether you consider that statement true or false.

WHAT IT LOOKS LIKE: There are several forms of the true-false question. They look like this:

A. Straight form: George Washington was the first president of the United States. _____.

Here the words true or false are to be written in after the statement.

B. Circle form:

T F George Washington was the first president of the United States.

Here you circle the T or F, or underline them, or check them, or in some other positive way mark your choice.

C. Cross-out form: Here the question looks the same as the circle form shown above: T F George Washington was the first president of the United States.

However, in this test, the instructions for the test indicate that you should cross out the wrong choice, rather than mark the right choice. Here, for example, you would cross out the F, rather than underline the T.

174

It is essential that you read the instructions thoroughly at the beginning of every test, to avoid any confusion between these two types of true-false choices. A single overlooked word here can ruin an entire year of study.

D. Separate-answer-sheet form:

Here the question is written on one paper, and space for the answer is given on a separate answer sheet, which is usually graded by a machine.

Each question and answer are, of course, numbered, and look like this:

On the question sheet:

17. George Washington was the first president of the

United States. On the answer sheet:

TF 17.| | | |

With such a test, neatness and precision again become crucial. It is incredible how many people lose grades on such tests, simply because they place the right answer in the wrong space. It is your job to make sure that such waste can never happen with you.

HOW TO MASTER IT

A true-false question is either completely right or it's wrong. In other words, every single word in the question must be utterly true, or the entire question is false. If there is one exception to a statement, the entire statement is false.

Therefore every word counts. One tiny word, anywhere in the statement, can turn it from true to false. Here, precision reading pays off. You should underline the key words of each statement in this way:

Harry S. Truman, born in Independence, Missouri, was 33rd president of the United States.

Here are two key facts that must be true to make statement true. Truman must have been the 33rd president of the United States, not the 32nd or 34th. And he must have been born in Independence, not in Saint Louis or Kansas City.

Since the second statement is false – since President Truman was not born in Independence – the question is answered false.

The procedure for answering a true-false question, therefore, is this:

1. Read the statement carefully. 2. Read it again, underlining the key words. 3. Determine whether each keyword, each key fact, is true or false. 4. If any key fact is wrong, the statement is wrong.

Only if all the key facts are correct can the statement be true.

WHAT TO WATCH OUT FOR In a true-false test you should always be suspicious of flat

statements that allow no exceptions. They are probably false. Tips-offs include such words as:

All Never Always Invariably

No None None Every

Any Absolutely

When you see such a word in a true-false question, automatically mark it false unless you are absolutely sure that there is no exception to the rule.

On the other hand, the following moderate words in a true-false question are usually tip-offs that the question is true:

Usually On the average Some Many Often

When you encounter such words, mark the question true, unless you find a key fact later in the statement that twists it false.

TYPE OF SHORT-ANSWER QUESTION 2: MULTIPLE CHOICE

DEFINITION: The multiple-choice test lists a number of possible answers after each of its questions. One of these answers is right; the rest are wrong. It is your task to choose the correct one.

WHAT IT LOOKS LIKE: The multiple-choice question may list its answers on the same line as the question itself, like this:

1. American Fighter planes are usually armed with machine guns of 22 30 32 45 50 57 calibre.

Or it may list the answers on separate lines, like this:

2. An efficient student –

- Studies with the radio volume lowered. =
- Studies at least two hours for every hour spent in class each week. =
- Does most of his reviewing just prior to an examination. =

- d. Does not make notations in his textbook.

It may list the answers as part of an incomplete statement, as in the examples as part of an incomplete statement, as in the examples above. Or it may ask a complete question, with separate answers listed below it, like this:

3. Which of the following is not an effective study habit.

- Studying in the same place each day.
- Revising notes immediately after lectures.
- Having a separate notebook for each class.

HOW TO MASTER IT

Whatever its form. The multiple-choice question forces you to choose and reject. And it does not make this choice easy. In fact, it often deliberately confuses, by furnishing answers that are designed to look near correct, and thus throw off the track.

For example, take this question from a vocabulary test. It asks you to choose the definition that is nearest in meaning to the first capitalized word.

4. IMPOSTURE – A: excessive burden. B: stooping position. C: fraud. D: handicap.

In this case, the correct answer is C: fraud. But there are two deliberately misleading clues in the question designed to draw you away from that correct answer, if you do not know it thoroughly.

The first is A: excessive burden, which is a definition of IMPOSITION, a word similar to imposture.

178

The second is B: stooping position, which plays on a possible misreading of the – POSTURE part of the question word.

Because of these built-in traps, a definite step-by-step technique is essential in answering multiple-choice questions. Let's examine that technique, right now:

STEP ONE: ANTICIPATE THE ANSWER

In multiple-choice questions like examples 1 and 4 above, where the question or incomplete-statement part makes sense by itself alone, without your reading on to the list of possible answers, do this:

FIRST: Read the first part of the question (for example, in 4, just the word IMPOSTURE) and then stop.

Second: Before you go on to the side of the paper what you believe is the correct answer.

(For example, you may immediately realize that IMPOSTURE means fakery or fraud. Or you may associate it with IMPOSTOR, a man who is a fraud. Lightly sketch the idea of fraud next to the answer, and then go on with the next step.)

THIRD: Then look for what you believe is the correct answer among the list of possible answers printed on the test.

(For example, when you C: fraud in the list of answers, you can be almost certain that you have it right.)

So your procedure in Step One – anticipating the answer – is first to read the question part of the statement, then jot down what you think is the correct answer, then look for that correct answer in the list of possible answers that completes the question.

Now, in examples 2 and 3 above, this technique must be altered slightly. Here the question part does not make sense by itself (for example, in 2 it says: "An efficient student – ")

Therefore you must read on, over each of the possible answers, making a light pencil check mark on the answer you believe is correct as soon as you read it.

(For example, as you read on to

1. Studies with the radio volume lowered. Which you do not believe is correct. So you go it:
2. Studies at least two hours for every hour spent in class.

This you believe is the correct answer. So you check it lightly as your first choice, and go on to second step, which is:

STEP TWO: READ EVERY POSSIBLE ANSWER

Now, once you have anticipated what you believe is the correct answer, you must make absolutely sure that you are right. You do this by a process of checking and elimination.

To begin this check, you now read every possible answer on the list.

(For example, in example 2 above, you go on to read:

3. Does most of his reviewing just prior to an examination. And also read:
4. Does not make notations in his textbook.)

STEP THREE: ELIMINATE THE WRONG ANSWERS

Now, as you read each of these other possible answers, you eliminate them one by one as being incorrect. Only when you have rejected all other answers except the correct one - only when you have proved to yourself that they are wrong – can you be certain that your choice is absolutely right.

To do this, you must give yourself a reason why each rejected answer is wrong. Let's see how you do this in example 2 above:

1. Studies with the radio volume lowered.

You immediately reject this answer as wrong, because the good student does not have the radio on when he studies at all. You then read:

2. Does most of his reviewing is a continuous process, starting the first day of study. And then you finish the list by reading:
3. Does not make notations in his textbook. Which is again wrong because the good student will underline in his textbook the essence of each chapter before he transfers that essence to his notebook.

You have now cross-checked your answer. You have anticipated the one correct answer; you have read all the others; and you have rejected them as wrong. You are now sure you are right.

STEP FOUR: MARK DOWN THE CORRECT ANSWER

You then mark down this correct answer, and go one to the next question.

HOW YOU CAN MAKLE A MULTIPLE-CHOICE QUESTION HELP YOU FIND THE CORRECT ANSWER IF YOURE NOT SURE OF IT YOURSELF

If you are well prepared, the technique outlined above will make you absolutely certain that you absolutely certain that you have the correct answer to over 90 per cent of all multiple-choice questions.

However, there will always be a question or two in every test where you are not sure of the correct answer. You may be confused; you may have temporarily forgotten it; you may need just a slight nudge to regain it again.

In this case, the question itself may help you clear up this confusion and point the way to the correct answer. Let's examine some of the techniques by which you can use the structure of make-up of that question to help you find the correct answer.

ELIMINATE THE WRONG ANSWERS FIRST

In most multiple-choice questions, you may not be sure which of the possible answers is correct, but you probably can tell that some of them are definitely wrong. In this case, since it is easier to choose among two answers that you know are wrong.

(For example, in 4 above, you may be confused between whether IMPSTURE is A: an excessive burden or C: a fraud.

182

But you are sure that it is not B: a stooping position or D: a handicap. So you eliminate thee two possibilities, and thus focus your attention on the two remaining possibilities, to which you now apply the following techniques.

REPRASE THE QUESTION

Often the memory-prod you need to come up with the right answer can be furnished by rephrasing the question. By turning a positive question into a negative one, by turning a noun asked for into a verb, or any other way of gaining a new slant on the question.

For example, in 4 above, instead of wrestling with IMPOSTURE, the act of defrauding, you may try changing the word into IMPOSTOR, a person who defrauds. Here you have a word that is far more familiar to you and that immediately clears up any question you might have had about whether the word could mean an excessive burden.

In the same way, in example 3 above, if you were torn between answers 2 and 3, you would rephrase the question in this way:

Which of the following IS an effective study habit? 2. Revising notes immediately after class? YES. 3. Having a separate notebook for each class? No. The answer becomes obvious immediately. By simply stating the OPPOSITE to the original question asked, the correct answer is thrown into clear focus.

TRY TO ELIMINATE EXTREMES.

Some multiple-choice questions, such as example 1 above, will have a scale of answers. This question asks you to complete the statement:

American fighter planes are usually armed with machine guns of 22 30 32 45 50 54 calibre.

On scale questions like this one, if you are not certain of the correct answer at once, you should start to work on the question by trying to eliminate the 22 and 54 calibre extremes. In most cases, these will be incorrect, and will leave you only four possible answers to choose from, rather than six.

LOOK FOR INTERNAL CLUS.

Many multiple-choice questions help you answer them, simply because of their construction. In some cases this construction eliminates certain possible answers; in others it points almost directly to the correct answer. Let us look at an example of each.

Which of the following were in part results of the immigration policy of the United States during the latter half of the nineteenth century? 1 – supply of cheap labour. 2 – growth of urban populations. 3 – opposition of organized labour to immigration policy. 4 – decline in birth rate.

(A) 1 and 2 only. (B) 1 and 3 only. (C) 1,2 and 3 only. (D) 1,2 and 4 only. (E) 1,2,3and 4.

Notice that all five possible answers include result 1- supply of cheap labour. Therefore, instantly, you can assume that this answer is correct, and use it as a test-furnished clue to help you choose the correct answer from the other choices.

In this case, of course, the fact that the immigration policy increased the supply of labour also meant that it increased the growth of urban populations, and that it naturally produced an opposition of organized labour to this incoming cheap-labour supply. It did not, however, decrease in any way the birth rate, but probably raised it.

There, by using the first possible correct answer as a clue, and logically applying its information to the remaining answers, you pulled out the final answer, even thought you did not know that answer when you first read the question.

The same technique of making the question furnish its own answer applies in the following example:

The action of "A Tale of Two Cities" takes place in:

1- Glasgow and London
2- New York and Paris
3- Vienna and Rome
4- Paris and London
5- Dublin and Edinburgh

Here you simply notice that only two cites are mentioned twice in the list of possible answers – Paris and London. Since these cities are mentioned twice – once together and once each with a third city to catch the unwary or careless student – it's highly probable that they are the correct answers. Which they are.

LOOK FOR SIGNS OF EXTRA CARE

Finally, if you are stumped on a multiple-choice question, you should always check to see if one of the possible answers is longer, or in a different vocabulary, or in any other way has had extra care spent on it, than the other answers in the list. If it has, this is a definite clue that it might be the correct answer.

For example, take this question from a test on chemistry:

The burning of gasoline in an automobile involves all of the following EXCEPT

(A) reduction
(B) decomposition
(C) an exothermic reaction
(D) oxidation
(E) conversion of matter to energy

Here two separate signs of extra care coincide to point out answer (E) as the correct one. First, it is much longer than the other answers Second it uses a different vocabulary – talking in plain English rather than technical terms.

These two clues should lead you to strongly suspect that answer (E) is the one you are looking for. Which it is.

Of course, all these techniques of making the question help you answer it are merely supplements to your preparation and knowledge. Ideally, they should be used merely to help you check the fact that you know the right answer, or as memory prods to help you over a temporary block in retrieving that answer from your storehouse of knowledge. They are never substitutes for study or ability.

A NOTE OF THE MASTERY OF MULTIPLKE_CHOICE QUESTIONS IN VOCABULARY TESTS

Most vocabulary tests – and they are extremely important to your progress in both social and business life are phrased in the form of multiple-choice questions.

These questions will either ask for synonyms (words that mean the same as the given word) or antonyms (words that mean the opposite of the given word). The synonym question is given in example 4 above. An antonym question is given in the example below:

Choose the lettered word which is most clearly OPPOSITE in meaning to the word in capital letters.

UNFIT: (A) tight (B) qualified (c) chosen (d) serene (E) necessary.

Such an antonym question is really two questions in one, and deserves a special technique of its own to solve it.

Here it is:

STEP ONE: THINK OF A SYNONYM FOR THE WORD

The moment you read the capitalized word, you should stop without reading on. Before you look at the list of possible answers, you should jot down your synonym. For example, in this case, you might think of not fit, incapable unqualified.

STEP TWO: THINK OF THE OPPOSITE OF THAT SYNONYM

Now – again before you read the list possible answers, jot down the opposite of your synonym on your paper. You might write, fit, capable, qualified.

STEP THREE: READ THE ANSWER LIST, AND ELIMINATE AND CHOOSE

Now read each possible answer in turn, comparing it with your own idea. You reject tight; are delighted to find the exact word you had anticipated, qualified, as the second possible answer, then go on to eliminate chosen, serene and necessary as a final check.

In this step-by-step way, such problems become simple, and confusion and trickery are both side-stepped. One more clue to help you solve these vocabulary tests. The word you are looking for in an answer list should be the same grammatical term as the have given, capitalized word.

If the given word is a noun, the correct answer should be a noun. If the given word is a verb, the correct answer should be a verb. And so on.

If, on the other hand, one of the possible answers is a different grammatical term (for instance, a verb when the given word is a noun), then it should be automatically eliminated as incorrect.

TYPE OF SHORT-ANSWERED QUESTION 4: ENUMERATION

DEFINITION: An enumeration question asks you to list a number of series of facts. It does not require the list to be given in any set order. It usually begins with the words list or name.

WHAT IT LOOKS LIKE: For example: List the members of the President's cabinet

HOW TO MASTER IT Here again, preparation is critical. If you know that you will be given enumeration questions on test, prepare for them by:

1. Making up such questions on your review self-examinations. And make sure that you get all the items in the series down on the paper.
2. In a series enumeration question, number the items in the series. Thus, if you know that there are ten members of the President's cabinet, you will not list only nine on your exam paper by mistake, and forget to put in the tenth.

TYPE OF SHORT-ANSWER QUESTION 5: SEQUENCE

DEFINITION: A sequence question asks you to list a series of acts in their proper order. Usually this will be the order in which historical events happened.

Or, as a combination of the sequence and multiple choice type of questions, you may be supplied with a list of events and asked to number them according to time.

WHAT IT LOOKS LIKE: The first form would be as simple as this:

List the first five Presidents of the Presidents of the United States in the order that they held office.

The second form would look like this: Number the following events in order of sequence.

- Congress of Berlin.
- Monroe Doctrine.
- Boxer Rebellion.
- Mexican War.

HOW TO MASTER THEM In dealing with the second form, there are two to follow:

1. Look for the first and last items of the series and number first. Then look for the second and next-to-last items. And so on. In this way, you are again getting rid of extremes first. And in this way narrowing down your area of choice and possibilities of making a mistake.
2. Number those items of which you are sure first. With a long list, you should take a piece of scratch paper, and re-create the list on it, putting down the items of which you are sure in their proper positions, and then simply using the other items to fill in the gaps. TYPE OF SHORT-ANSWER QUESTION 6: MATCHING DEFINITION: A matching question usually consists of two lists of items placed side by side. You are required to match the items on one list with the items on the other, by marking the numbers from the list in the spaces provided in front of the second.

WHAT IT LOOKS LIKE: Write the letter of each of the cities front of the state of which it is the capital.

- South Dakota
- Kentucky
- California
- Nevada
- Nebraska

A. Frankfort B. Pierre
C. Omaha
D. Sacramento
E. Carson City

HOW TO MASTER IT

Again, elimination of known answers is the key. There are two quick methods of doing this:

1. Run light pencil lines between those items on the first and second lists that you are absolutely sure of.
2. Cross off an item in the second list as soon as you mark its letter on the first list.

In this way you eliminate the sure answers first and are able to concentrate your attention on the one or two remaining items that needs more prodding without being confused.

Here again, you must remember that tests also teach. They give information as well as demand it. Many clues are contained in a matching question that will help you pull out the correct answer.

For example, in the question above, you may not know that Carson City is the capital of Nevada, but you may know that it is a city in that state. The mere fact that it is mentioned in a list of state capitals then tells you all you need to know to answer the question correctly.

TYPE OF SHORT-ANSWER QUESTION 7: CROSS OUT

DEFINITION: A cross-out question is one that asks you to eliminate the wrong item in a series. For example:

WHAT IT LOOKS LIKE: Cross out the numbers that do not being in the following series:

5 10 20 40 50 60 80 160 320

HOW TO MASTER IT

Cross-out questions are difficult for most students because they are really two-part questions and must be done one part at a time. If you try to do both parts at the same time, or just plunge hopelessly into question an organized technique, you will become immediately lost.

With technique, however, the cross-out question is really simple. Here is the proper procedure:

STEP ONE: DEFINE WHAT IS HAPPENING IN THE SERIES

The first thing you must do when you encounter a series of numbers is to find out what is going on in that series. Are the numbers increasing or decreasing? Is another number being added to them? If so, how big is that number? Or are they doubling, or tripling, or halving? What is the principle that determine what the next number will be?

For example, in the series above, you start by asking "What happens to 5 that makes it 10?" There are two answers: Either 5 more is added to it, or it is doubled.

You next go on to the relation between 10 and 20. You ask yourself: "What happens to 10 that makes it 20? Again there are two possible answers: Either 10 more is added to it, or it is doubled.

Now you have a pattern. The number 5 was doubled to make 10, and 10 was doubled to make 20.You now believe that you know what is going on in the series: each number is doubled to make the next.

You now test this pattern on the next number. It is 10. The number 20 is doubled to make 40, so it fits. The pattern still holds.

If the pattern is correct, the next number should be 80. But it's 50 instead. So you go on to:

STEP TWO: LOCATE THE WRONG ITEMS AND CROSS THEM OUT

The number 50 does not follow the double pattern, so you put a light line through it – to indicate that you believe for the moment that it should be crossed out – and go on to the next number.

This number is 60. Again, it doesn't fit the double pattern. And again you put a light line through it and go on to the next number.

This number is 80. Here the pattern takes over again. You have expected 80, and found it. This indicates that both 50 and 60 were wrong numbers and should be crossed out.

But, to make certain, you still have two remaining number to check out the problem. You now test each of them.

The next number is 160. The number 80doubled is 160. The pattern fits.

The next number is 320. The number 160 doubled is 320. Again the pattern fits.

You are now certain that 50 and 60 are the wrong numbers. You cross them out and go on to the next question.

This same two-part technique will be used to solve the "terror of test-rooms," which is:

TYPE OF SHORT_ANSWER QUESTION 8: NUMBER SERIES

DEFINITION: The number-series question presents you with a series of numbers again, but this time all are correct, and you are required to write down the next one or two numbers at the end of the series.

WHAT IT LOOKS LIKE: A number-series question is usually presented in groups, starting with easy ones, and ending up with the very difficult. Here is a sample you might find on any mathematical-aptitude test:

1. 591317212529—
2. 40302010–
3. 61854162486—
4. 7101415182223–
5. 37597119--
6. 1289146203–
7. 24839274--

HOW TO MASTER IT

Again, every number-series question is a two-part question. Its first part must be solved first before you can begin to answer it finally.

Here are the two questions you must answer before you can solve any number-series question:

1. What is happening in this series? What kind of progression is going on?
2. What, then, must the next one or two numbers in this series be?

The first question must be answered correctly before you can answer the second. Therefore your first job in attacking any number-series question is to discover and mark down the series pattern.

In fact, it is so important that you thoroughly understand this pattern that you actually mark it down on your test paper like this:

In example 1 above, you ask yourself, "What happens to 5 that makes it 9?" The answer is that 4 is added to it, and you draw a line between the 5 and the 9 and mark down +4 on top of that line, like this:

+4 5----9

Now you ask yourself, "What happens to 9 that makes it 13?" The answer is again plus 4. And you again draw a line between the two numbers and mark +4 above it like this:

+4 +4 5----9----13

A physical, concrete pattern that you can see is now beginning to emerge before your eyes. You continue this marking of the pattern through every number in the series, until, when you have finished the first step, the question now looks like this:

+4 +4 +4 +4 +4 +4 5----9----13----17----21----25----29---

The pattern is now obvious. To answer the second part of the question, you simply add 4 to 29 to get 33, and then add 4 again to get 37.

This same technique of marking the pattern is now obvious. To answer the second part of the question, you simply add 4 to 29 to get 33, and then add 4 again to get 37.

This same technique of marking the pattern greatly simplified all number-series questions. In example 2, for instance, the pattern – 10 emerges, and the problem looks like this:

-10 -10 -10 40----30----20----10---

At this point, the answer quite obviously becomes 0.

In example 3, the pattern x3 emerges, and the problem looks like this:

X3 X3 X3 X3 6----18----54----162----486

The answers thus become 1,458 and 4,374. But, in example 4, the pattern becomes more complicated. In examples 1,2 and 3, the same pattern held for every number in the series. In example 1, the pattern +4 held for every number. In example 2, the pattern -10 held for every number. And in example 3, the pattern x3 held for every number.

But in example 4, no one pattern holds throughout the series. The pattern between the first two minutes looks like this:

+3 7----10

The pattern between the second two numbers emerges like this:

+3 +4 7----10----14

And the pattern between the third two numbers looks like this:

+3 +4 +1 7----10----14----15

So far there is no relation between these two-number patterns. But in the next two numbers, this pattern emerges:

+3+4 +1 +3 +4 7----10----14----15----18----22

It is, of course. And the final number should then be 23, to give this final look to the problem.

+3 +4 +1 +3 +4 +1 7----10----14----15----18----22----23

The overall pattern has now emerged. It is a repeat of +3 +4 +1. Therefore, it is obvious that the next number in the series, the final answer, is obtained by adding 3 to 23 to get 26.

What you have encountered here is a pattern composed of three different numbers, all of which are added in rotation to the numbers that occur in the series.

This new pattern is more complicated then the patterns in the first three examples, each of which are added in rotation to the number (4, 10 and 3, and one operation (addition, subtraction, and multiplication).

Example 4, however, though it had only one operation (addition) had three numbers.

Now, what happen if you were given a number series with two operations and two numbers?

This example

5. Writing in the pattern, you get this:

+4 -2+4-2 +4 -2 3----7----5----9----7----11----9---

The answer becomes obvious at once. Adding 4 to 9, you get 13. And subtracting 2 from 13, you get 11.

In a number series, there can be any number of operations and any number of numbers to perform them on.

But number series can get even more complicated. Take example 6. Marking in our single pattern, we get this:

-4 +1 +5 -8 +14 -17 12----8----9----14----6----20-----3

Here, there seems to be no pattern at all. And there is no single pattern. For a number series can also have more than one pattern. For a number series can also have more than one pattern in it. It can have two or more patterns.

But where are these patterns? Certainly not between the first and second or second and third numbers.

Then why not experiment? Why not try the first and third numbers, and then the third and fifth? And then the second and fourth numbers, and fourth and sixth?

If you try this, here is how your first every-other-number pattern will look:

__-3____ __-3____ _ __-3__ 12----8----9----14----6----20----3

And here's how your second every-other-number pattern now looks:

__-3_ ___-3__ ___-3__ 12----8----9----14----6----20----3 +6 +6

Now the patterns have emerged, and the answer is again obvious. You add 6 to 20 and get correct answer, 26.

And once you get used to the idea of two or more patterns in a single number series, even the most complicated problems of this type become a snap. In example 7, for instance, you immediately spot the pattern as being this:

x2 x2 x3 x3 x4 x4 2----4----8 3----9----27 4----

You simply multiply 4 by 4 to get 16, and 16 by 4 to get 64, and you have the correct answer.

Again, as in all these number series problems, the two step technique works miracles in making the answer emerge. First, you discover the pattern. Then the pattern tells you the next number you need to complete the series.

TYPE OF SHORT-ANSWER QUESTION 9: ANALOGIES

DEFINITION: AN Analogy question asks you to compare one relation between two objects to another, similar relation between two other objects. Its usual form is "this is to that as something is to something else".

WHAT IT LOOKS LIKE: Knowledge is to judgment as possession is to (1) law (2) acquisition (3) use (4) ignorance (5) dispassion.

Or, in a slightly different form: HOURGLASS: CLOCK is most similar to:

(1) acorn: oak (2) foundation: temple (3) temple: church (4) catapult: church (5) catapult: cannon.

HOW TO MASTER IT

Again, like the number-series question, the analogy question is composed of two parts, one of which is stated and other hidden.

The first step in solving an analogy question is to find, and state, the relation between the two objects that are given.

The second step is to choose the two objects in the answer list that have the same relation as the given objects.

First, you find the relation between the two given objects, and write it down just as you wrote down the hidden pattern in the number-series questions. Then you find the other pair of objects in the answer list that have exactly the same relation.

For example, what is the relation between HOUR GLASS and CLOCK?

An hourglass is a PRIMITIVE clock. It was the FORE RUNNER of the clock. So this PRIMITIVE, FOREUNNER relation is what you are locking for. You write it down and begin testing each of the pairs in the answer list against it.

Acorn oak. Not quite the same. An oak grows from an acorn, but a clock replaces an hourglass. The oak was inherent in the acorn, but a clock is an entirely different mechanism from an hourglass. Mark it no and go on.

Foundation: temple. No resemblance in the relation. A temple is built on a foundation, but a clock is not built in any way on the same foundation as an hourglass. No.

Temple: church. No. Two different houses of worships. Both exist at the present time. No resemblance.

Catapult: church. No comparison.

Catapult: cannon. This looks like it. A catapult is a PRIMITIVE cannon, just as an hourglass was a PRIMITIVE clock. A catapult was a FORERUNNER of the cannon, just as the hourglass was a FORERUNNER of the clock. This is the correct answer. You mark it down and go on to the next question.

What is the relation between KNOWLEDGE and JUDGMENT? To put the same technique to work:

Knowledge is a REQUIREMENT for good judgment. To be a good judge, one must have knowledge. This is the relation you are looking for. You write it down – a REQUIREMENT – and begin testing the pairs in the answer list again it.

Possession: law. Possession is not a requirement for law. No resemblance.

Possession: acquisition. Possession is not a requirement for acquisition. They are practically synonymous. No resemblance.

Possession: use. Possession is a requirement for use. You must possess something to use it. This looks like the correct answer. You check it off, but still go on to each of the other possibilities to make absolutely certain.

Possession: ignorance. No resemblance at all.

Possession: dispossession. No resemblance. They mean exactly the opposite.

Therefore it must be possession: use. The correct answer emerges, once the hidden relation is brought out into the open.

TYPE OF SHORT-ANSWER QUESTION 10: THE COMBINATION QUESTION

Finally, of course, many of the questions you will encounter on your examinations will be combinations of one or two of the types described above.

These combination questions can always be solved by the step-by- step method. They are first broken down into the number of steps it takes to solve them, and then each step is done in its turn.

For example, take this question from a typical geography quiz:

Select the third letter of the word which correctly completes the following statement: Chicago is located in the state of

(1) – I (2) – A (3) – N (4) – L (5) – O

There are two parts to this question. First, to find the state in which Chicago is located, which is Illinois. Then, to find the third letter of the word, Illinois, which is - L. Thus the correct answer is 4.

Though the question may have seemed hard or confusing when you first encountered it, it becomes simple as soon as you break it down step by step.

A FINAL NOTE ON A VERY SPECIAL TYPE OF TEST: HOW TO RAISE YOUR I.Q.

Throughout your career you will be judged by, not one, but two separate systems of grading you.

The first system, of course, will be your results in exams you are given – for a better job, more pay, advanced degree, and all the others we have mentioned.

The second system of grading you will be your results in the I.Q tests you will be given from time tom time. For example, as a routine measure by large companies when you apply for a new job with them.

There is nothing mysterious or Godlike or absolutely final about an I.Q test. It is just another kind of test. What it measured is not really your innate intelligence's, but simply your ability to pass this type of test.

Therefore, as in other test, your grades can be improved by planning and practice. And, since this probably the most important single test you will ever take in your career, let us right now examine each one of the types of questions you will encounter on it, and how you can improve your performance on them:

1. Synonyms. Select the word which means the same.

Sample:

BABY:

1. son
2. child;
3. sister;
4. born.

Technique:

1. Think of our synonym before you read the list. 2. Read the entire list, crossing out wrong possibilities, and matching your answer to the answer to the answer on the list.
2. Antonyms. Select the word which means the opposite.

Sample: Back: 1. side; 2. front; 3.top.

Technique: 1. Think of our synonym before you read the list. 2. Think of the

word that means exactly the opposite. 3. Read the entire answer list to find this word and cross out the others.

3. Classification. Verbal cross-outs. Cross out the word that does not belong with the others.

Sample: A. daisy; B. rose; C. cat; D. lily

Technique:

1. Read the entire list to discover the –all classification.
2. Write down the name of the classification.
3. Go over every word, crossing out the one does not belong.

Warning:

Beware of the first word on the list. It may be the wrong one. Therefore read the entire list before deciding on the over-all classification.

4. Logical reasoning. Special type of multiple choice. Select the word which tells what the first word always has.

Sample: BOOK: A. pictures; B. pages; C. cover; D. story.

Warning:

Key word here is always. Not sometimes or may possibly. But always – without fail. Therefore, even though a book may sometimes have pictures, or a cover, or a story, it only has, without fail, pages, or it could not be a book.

Technique:

1. Ask immediately, before reading the list, "A book could only be a book, without fail, if it had - -." 2. Write down the answer. 3. Read the entire list, matching your own answer, and crossing out the other possibilities as they do not fit.

5. Number sequence. Filling in the next number in a given series.

Sample:

What number should come next? 2 4 6 8 10 12 –

Technique:

1. Find out what happens in the series – establish the pattern between each of the numbers in the series. 2. Use this pattern to show you the next number.

6. Analogies. Given two objects with a specific relation, find a similar relation in two other objects.

Sample:

Gun is to shoot as knife is to: A. fly; B. meat; C. hurt; D. cut; E. hit.

Technique:

Again, use two steps. 1 Define the relation between the two given objects, and write it down. 2. Find the same relation between one of the possible answers, eliminating each of the others as you read it.

7. Proverbs. A kind of analogy. Given a famous proverb, find another statement among those furnished which means the same or most nearly the same.

Sample: DO NOT HANG ALL ON ONE NAIL. A. Don't count your chickens until they're hatched. B. Don't put all your eggs in one basket. C. Don't use a nail, use a hanger.

Technique:

1. After reading the given proverb, before you read the answer
   list, try to rephrase it in more general terms (for instance, in
   this sample, try: "Don't risk all on one chance").
2. Read each of the possibilities, to find the one that matches
   your own rephrasing. These, then, are the seven most types
   of questions given on I.Q tests. To get the top possible
   grades you are capable of getting on these tests, go over
   these types of questions again and again. Make up new
   examples. Be sure you can use the right technique on each
   of them as easily as you can write your own name.

IN SUMMARY:

You will encounter these ten types of short-answer question on your tests:

True- false. Multiple-choice. Completion. Matching. Enumeration.

Analogies. Number series. Cross out. Sequence. Combinations.

Through applying the proper techniques, each of these questions can be made simple, and even help to furnish all or part of its own answer.

By giving yourself practice, and more practice in solving each of them, you will turn yourself into a test-room champion.

CHAPTER 18
How to master the essay test

The second great category of test that you will have to deal with in the examination room is the essay test.

The essay test requires you to write. It confronts you with a question, or a series of questions, that demand lengthy, organized answers that may take up a full written page or more.

It tests you ability to:

1. Organize your ideas, and
2. Express them clearly and logically on paper.

Therefore, on the essay test, you are graded on tow accomplishments:

1. What you say and
2. How you say it.

Let us see how to get better grades in both these areas.

THE BASIC STRATEGY IN TAKING AN ESSAY TEST

We will, of course, assume that you have prepared for the test in the manner outlined in this book. In other words, that you have absorbed and organized the material, arranged it in notes, reviewed the note to eliminate any misunderstandings, and, above all, quizzed yourself on the information in those notes by creating and answering a series of essay- type questions of your own.

Because of this preparation, then, when you enter the exam room you are ready, not only with thoroughly organized material, but with some of the very questions that you will be asked on the test.

With this bedrock background, you follow this procedure:

1. First read the complete list of questions. In some essay exams, only one or two or three questions may make up the entire test. In others, there may be as many as ten questions, each demanding only a paragraph or two.

In any case, carefully read them all, asking yourself these two primary questions:

"Do I have to answer all the questions that are asked on this test, or does the test give me a choice?"

"Either way, how many questions will I have to answer in the time I have allotted for this test?"

2. Let us say, for example, that there are five essay questions that you must answer on this test. Once you have determined this fact, you now proceed to ration your time.

You do it in this way:

Determine the total amount of time you will have for the test – let us say two hours, or one hundred and twenty minutes. First allow yourself twenty minutes at the end of this two hours, to review what you have written and to correct any errors that you might have overlooked the first time.

This leaves you with one hundred minutes of writing, in which you will have to answer five questions. Therefore in you allot twenty minutes to each question.

You now have your over-all time schedule set up. Now turn to the individual questions.

3. If the test does not demand that you do the question in a specific order, arrange them in order yourself. Do the easiest question first. The second-easiest second, and so on.
4. Now, each individual question gets its own time schedule. Each of these answers has two steps:

First it is outlined. Then it is written. The outline is easily as important as the final written answer. It is in this outline that you build the idea backbone of your answer. That you organize the thoughts that you will later put sentences.

Therefore, for each answer you should take about one fifth of your time to outline the answer, and the rest to write it out on the basis of that outline.

For example, four minutes to outline your answer and sixteen minutes of guided writing will give you a far better grade than a mere twenty minutes of blind writing. And the organization of your thought will shines right through.

And, above all, this way you won't write yourself into a corner, where you find you're just beginning to answer the question when the exam time is almost over.

Now, let's take a look at some of the essay questions you will be required to answer, and what you must do to get each of them precisely right.

THE KEY ESSAY-QUESTION WORDS, AND HOW TO ANSWER EACH OF THEM CORRECTLY

KEY WORD: 1. Evaluate   SAMPLE QUESTION: Evaluate the concept of "over learning" as a sound study procedure.

WHAT TO DO TO ANSWER IT CORRECTLY: An evaluation is an appraisal, a weighing of pros and cons.

Therefore your answer should cite the advantages and disadvantages of the subject being discussed, and end with your opinion of its worth.

KEY WORD: 2. Summarize SAMPLE QUESTION:

Summarize the main economic causes of World War 1. WHAT TO DO TO ANSWER IT CORRECTLY:

A summary is a condensed outline of main points. Therefore you should give the main points only in a concise, outline form, omitting minor detail. Here, the bare outline will often do for the answer, if you are in a hurry.

KEY WORD: 3. Compare SAMPLE QUESTION: Compare standardized and teacher-made tests in respect to use in the classroom. WHAT TO DO TO ANSWER IT CORRECTLY:
A comparison is an examination of character or qualities, for the purpose of discovering resemblances or differences. Therefore you should first list the qualities of each of the two subjects to be compared, and then show how they resemble each other, or how they differ from each other. You are not required to evaluate them, or end up with an opinion on their comparative worth.

KEY WORD: 4. Explain. SAMPLE QUESTION: Explain the concept of a chain reaction. WHAT TO DO TO ANSWER IT

CORRECTLY: To explain is to make plain. Therefore you should show exactly how the subject works, in logical, step-by-step order. This happens, which causes this to happen, which causes this to happen.

KEYWORD: 5. Criticize. SAMPLE QUESTION:

Criticize. The statement, "A firm should cut its advertising budget when its sales turn down." WHAT TO DO TO ANSWER IT CORRECTLY:

A criticism is an examination of a subject and then a judgment. Therefore you should first examine the evidence for and against the statement, and then give your opinion on its merits.

KEYWORD: 6. Name. SAMPLE QUESTION:

Name three factors that are basic to success in the stock market. WHAT TO DO TO ANSWER IT CORRECTLY: This is the easiest and shortest of all essay questions. Simply name the subjects asked for, without further detail.

KEYWORD: 7.Discuss. SAMPLE QUESTION: Discuss something is to examine it from all angles. Therefore you should give the complete story of the subject asked for, from its beginning to its end.

KEYWORD: 8. Outline. SAMPLE QUESTION: Outline the principal steps in preparing a sales report. WHAT TO DO TO ANSWER IT CORRECTLY: You have been outlining all year long. Therefore simply use your primary outline as the final answer to this question.

KEYWORD: 9. List. SAMPLE QUESTION: List five ways to increase the power of a stock Ford engine. WHAT TO DO

TO ANSWER IT CORRECTLY: A listing is simply a naming. Therefore number the subjects asked for, and name them one after the other without further elaboration.

KEYWORD: 10.Define. SAMPLE QUESTION: Define the term "expletive." WHAT TO DO TO ANSWER IT CORRECTLY: A definition is the explanation of the meaning of a word. Therefore start your definition with "An (expletive) is...," and explain its meaning in the remainder of the sentence. Few words will require more than one sentence.

KEYWORD: 11.State. SAMPLE QUESTION: State three reasons for Red China's being barred from the United Nations.

WHAT TO DO TO ANSWER IT CORRECTLY: To state is the same as to name. Therefore use the same procedure as that discussed above.

KEYWORD: 12.Review. SAMPLE QUESTION: Review the principal causes of the Stock Market crash of 1929. WHAT TO DO TO ANSWER IT CORRECTLY:

Same as discuss. Use same procedure.

KEYWORD: 13. Describe. SAMPLE QUESTION: Describe the circulatory system of the human body. WHAT TO DO TO ANSWER IT CORRECTLY: A description is simply a narration without searching for causes. Therefore simply follow through the process asked for, step by step, without giving any reasons for its cause or order.

KEYWORD: 14.Enumerate. SAMPLE QUESTION: Enumerate the results of Soviet Russia's walling off of East Berlin from the West.

WHAT TO DO TO ANSWER IT CORRECTLY: To enumerate is to list or name. Therefore use the technique described above.

KEYWORD: 15.Illustrate. SAMPLE QUESTION: Give three illustrations of President Eisenhower's foreign policy during his term of office.

WHAT TO DO TO ANSWER IT CORRECTLY: To illustrate is to give examples. Therefore name the number of examples required, describing them sufficiently to identify them, but neither evaluating them nor giving causes for their existence.

KEYWORD: 16.Interpret. SAMPLE QUESTION:

Interpret the Supreme Court ruling on integration in the University of Mississippi Case. WHAT TO DO TO ANSWER IT CORRECTLY: An interpretation is an explanation, usually in reference to a specific instance or view point. Therefore explain the consequence of the subject (in this case, the Supreme Court ruling) in the instance asked for (in this case, the University of Mississippi dispute.)

KEYWORD: 17.Justify. SAMPLE QUESTION: Justify the statement, "All behaviour is ultimately caused by circumstances outside the individual."

WHAT TO DO TO ANSWER IT CORRECTLY:

A justification is a marshaling of reasons for a cause or statement. Therefore list each of the facts that prove the statement given, and show how they combine to make it true,

KEYWORD: 18.Prove. SAMPLE QUESTION: What is the proof for the second law of thermodynamics? WHAT TO DO ANSWER IT CORRECTLY:

Proof is double evidence – first that a statement is correct, and second that an opposite statement must be false. Therefore list the facts that serve as evidence for the given statement, and then supplement them with further facts that disprove any contradictory statements.

KEYWORD: 19.Contrast. SAMPLE QUESTION: Contrast The General Motors and Ford approaches to the automotive market following World War II.

WHAT TO DO TO ANSWER IT CORRECTLY: To contrast two objects is to bring out their differences. Therefore list the differences between the two objects mentioned in the question, difference by difference. You are not required to list their similarities or evaluate them.

TIPS ON RAISING YOUR ANSWERS ABOVE THE ORDINARY LEVEL

Once you have identified the exact way you will respond to each key word, and outline your answer to each question, you then proceed to write out your answers on the test paper. To improve your grades you follow these simple rules:

5. You should not use handwriting tricks. Write clearly and neatly, with large indentions at the beginning of each paragraph.
6. For every answer, adopt a position and then stick to it. Third position should be declared in the first sentence of each answer in the way:

"Teacher-made tests are for superior to standardized tests for the following reasons:..."

7. Document each answer, where possible, with detailed supporting evidence. Once you have memorized your backbone facts, then many concrete details will be carried along in your memory with them. Use these details everywhere they occur, to be as specific as you can.

For example, you should not say: "Man needs a certain minimum daily food intake." If you have the information to say: "A man weighing 165 pounds needs as many as 4,500 calories per day."

8. Certain easy-to-do devices add great excitement and believability to your answers – make your examination paper stand out head and shoulders above the common crowd. Use as many of the following devices as possible:

- Diagrams.
- Graphs.
- Outlines.
- Underlined sections.
- Technical terms.
- Illustrations and examples.

9. Cross references save time, squeeze more information into each question, impress readers. They are a simple method of quoting part of one question to help document another.

For example, you might use a cross reference in this way:

"Teacher-made tests are also superior to the standard version for the reasons stated in answer 2 (b) and 3 (c) given above."

10. There is no reason for you to argue with position taken by the teacher in the exam statements. Take the teacher's position as your own and develop it as given.

11. Never use slang. Use good English and good logic throughout.

WHAT TO DO IN THE LAST TWENTY MINUTES

12. Save the last twenty minutes as a safety factor. When you reach them, stop writing, no matter how far along you are in the test.
13. If you have finished all the answers, you now carefully read them, correcting spelling and punctuation, checking them against your outline to make sure have included every main point.

If you wish to add a final idea, do so at the bottom of the question, beginning it with a statement such as: "One further point that increases the superiority of teacher- made tests even further..."

14. .If, however, you have not finished that "one last question," use half this twenty minutes to fill it in this way:

Make a formal outline of the answer. Touch on all aspects of the answer in this formal outline, using clear concise sentences for each main point. If your outline is valid and clear enough, and your other answers show a mature writing style, you may receive full credit for this outline answer as well.

15. Above all, use every second of time allowed by the test to make sure your answers are the absolute best you can make them.

In all these answers, give exactly what is called for. Neither more nor less than is expected. Clear, concise, to the point. And then go to the next question.

IN SUMMARY:

Essay tests are graded on two separate accomplishments:

Your ability to: 1. Organize ideas, and 2. Express them clearly and logically.

Therefore, to get top grades on an essay test, a plan of attack is essential.

One-fifth of your time should be devoted to outline your answers, three-fifths of your time to writing out those outline answers, and the remaining one-fifth of your time to checking and writing to remove any omissions or errors.

Each answer should give exactly what is called for in the question. Therefore you should exactly what is called for in the question. Therefore you should give exactly what is called the question. Therefore you should know what each essay test key word demands from you, and be immediately ready to satisfy it.

CHAPTER 19
The simple strategy of making the test help you pass it

Now that you are familiar with the types of questions that you will encounter in your tests, and have been drilled in the proper way to answer each of them, let us now bring all these test-taking skills together, and see how you use them to pull out a top grade in an actual examination.

We have already done this for an essay-type test. Now we will set up the same strategy – for the hundreds of short-answer tests you will take during your lifetime.

Here you go. On your way to another test-taking triumph. THE FIRST FIVE MINUTES

Your first goal, when you enter the room, is always to overcome whatever emotional excitement you may have brought with you. You want to take this test calmly and coolly, in complete charge of all the information you have prepared.

For this reason, the first five minutes are crucial. It is during these five minutes that you either settle yourself down to productive work, and make the test work for you, or give away to panic and mind-blocking. In order to avoid this, you follow this simple procedure:

1. Lay down your pencil on the desk, and do not pick it up for five minutes.
2. Use this five minutes to pre-read the exam. To be come familiar with the entire exam before you do any part of it. To read all directions twice. To look especially for the following points:

- What are the exact instructions? Are the answers to be given in any special way? Is there a choice of questions, or does every question have to be answered?
- Are there any questions that you anticipated? If so, they will give a big boost to your confidence.
- How long is the exam? Will there be a time problem? If so, start on the easiest or most familiar questions, skipping those you don't know and coming back to them later if you have the time.
- What parts of the exam give you the most credit? Do these first, if you them.
- Are there any questions that are closely related? If so, make sure you don't give the same answer on both.
- Do nay questions give the answer, or suggest the answer, to another question? This happens far too often to be overlooked, and can add as much as 10 per cent to 15 per cent to your grade.

3. All these pre-reading questions must be answered before you pick up your pen actually to begin writing the exam.

At this point you will be calm, confident, and deliberate, without trace of the emotional overexcitement that could spell disaster.

WRITING THE EXAM: HOW TO AVOID THE 20 PER CENT OF CARELESS ERRORS THAT MOST PEOPLE MAKE

In the actual writing of the exam, of course, the second great danger occurs. This is plain ordinary carelessness, the malady that causes more test failures than anything else but sheer neglect of study.

Here are some of the most frequent mistakes caused by nothing else but sheer carelessness:

You fail to read the question correctly. You miss key words, or miss their meaning.

You read only part of a question, and then start to answer without reading the rest of the question. But that last part of the question may change its meaning entirely.

You make a list when you're asked to explain. Or give incidents and events, rather than the causes for them. Or compare when you're asked to contrast. Or write long, detailed lists of reasons, when you're asked to give the main reason only.

Such patterns of carelessness are constant. When you develop one of them, you will repeat it over and over again, unless you stamp it out.

Therefore, as we have said before, study your particular pattern of carelessness BEFORE you get in the test room. And then correct it, day by day, till it is completely eradicated, and you will never slip back into it, even under the most extreme pressure.

WRITING THE EXAM: MAKING SURE THAT EACH ANSWER IS CORRECT

4. Now you pick up your pencil and begin to answer the test. Your first step is to go back to the questions you are sure of, and answer them first.
5. Use these correct answers, plus the information given you in the other test questions, plus the techniques of making questions solve themselves that we have described, to work through the remaining questions that you are not completely sure of.

6. Solve them one question at a time. Read each twice to make sure you understand it. Concentrate on it exclusively, without glancing at the remaining questions till you have finished it. Then go on to the next one.
7. Strive for neatness, good order, correct spelling grammar and punctuation where required.
8. Try to allot yourself five or ten minutes after you have finished the test to review it. Use this time to check back over the test to make sure there are no careless mistakes or omissions. Do not, however, "second-guess" your answers. Rely on your first intuitive answer unless you have uncovered new information further along in the test that makes you sure that you have a better answer.
9. If there are answers still unfinished, or questions you do not know, follow this rule: If the test does not penalize for guessing or wrong answers, and if an   unanswered question will be graded wrong, then make the best possible guess.

If, however, the test penalizes for guessing in any way, simply leave the questions blank.

10. Again, use every second of the time given to you by the test. Check and recheck to make sure you have made no correctible mistakes, no omissions that you have squeezed out the absolute top grade you are capable of.

And then hand the paper in and forget it. Because you know that you have done your job – done it well – and can confidently await your reward.

IN SUMMARY:

In taking any test, you must first concentrate on eliminating:

1. Overexcitement and emotional block.
2. Careless mistakes.

Once you have done this, you then concentrate on making one part of the test help you solve the other, as we have shown you in these chapters.

These three basic techniques add up to top grades on any test that can be thrown at you. Exercised properly, they give you an enormous advantage over any other person inn that test room.

EPILOGUE

How to make yourself into a mental champion

There it is. You now have the techniques you need to double your power to learn.

They are simple, fast, and enormously effective. Used properly, they can get the job you might have missed, the recognition and prestige that may have passed you by, the extra pay raises that might have otherwise slipped through your fingers – all the rewards in life that go only to the well-prepared, well-educated person who can use every drop of power of his brain is capable of.

But they can't do a darned one of these things without your active support!

Reading these techniques – even learning them – is just not enough. Teaching them to yourself is not enough. Even memorizing them is not enough.

They are good to you until they become SECOND NATURE! Until they are built into your nervous system as reaction patterns or habits. Until you do them automatically – perfectly – without thinking. As easily and quickly and naturally as you now write your name.

And this means PRACTICE! PRACTICE! PRACTICE!

Champions in any field, whether it be art, or sports, or business, or study, are made by two great tolls:

1. Knowledge or technique
2. Practice to perfect that technique.

The first element, knowledge, can be bought. It can be bought in the form of a book, or a lecture, or even in the form of hard experience.

But the second element, practice, can only be earned. It is a function of character. It is a result of that inner drive, persistence, endurance, patience, will to win, inability to quit that makes the champion.

In life, it is not intelligence that makes the great difference. We have all seen too many brilliant minds left panting behind – shattered and defeated – doomed to lives of nameless mediocrity.

In life, ultimately, it is drive that counts! The tortoise still wins; the hare still is left sleeping in obscurity!

"A winner never quits; a quitter never wins!" "Practice makes perfect."

This old wisdom. True wisdom. Wisdom that works today in the science laboratory as much as it did in the groves of Socratic Greece.

Teach it to yourself. Build into your brain, not only the techniques that produce success, but the drive that will settle for nothing less than success, and you will have learned the most powerful secret of success in the entire world! A secret that will open up an entire new world of accomplishment to you!

Good Luck! And Good Learning!

Made in the USA
Middletown, DE
12 April 2017